THE STORY OF PANTOMIME

MODERN PANTOMIME BOY: PAT KIRKWOOD LEADS IN THE CHORUS

The Story of Pantomime

by

A. E. WILSON

With a new introduction by

ROY HUDD

"Of all people children are the most imaginative; they abandon themselves without reserve to every illusion. Every image which is strongly presented to their mental eye produces in them the effect of reality. No man, whatever his sensibility may be, is ever affected by Hamlet or Lear as a little girl is affected by poor Red Riding Hood."

LORD MACAULAY.

EP Publishing Limited
Rowman and Littlefield
1974

This edition republished 1974 by
EP Publishing Limited
East Ardsley, Wakefield
Yorkshire, England
and in the United States of America by
Rowman & Littlefield
Totowa, New Jersey

ISBN 0 85409 967 0
(EP Publishing)

ISBN 0-87471-458-3
(Rowman and Littlefield)

Please address all enquiries to EP Publishing Limited
(address as above)

Printed in Great Britain by
Redwood Press Limited, Trowbridge, Wiltshire

DEDICATION

To my niece
TESSA WILSON
and all other pantomime-lovers
of her age

Contents

List of Illustrations

Introduction

by Roy Hudd

"What made you go on the stage?" . . . I should think every performer has been asked this question more times than any other, except perhaps for "Can I have your autograph?—it's not for me it's for my little girl". There are several stock answers to the first question. "I did it so I wouldn't have to get up in the morning", "It's better than working" or "Sssh! my Mum might find out—she thinks I'm in prison!".

However, seriously folks, nearly all my pals in show business will eventually come round to telling you that they first longed to tread the boards as a direct result of seeing their first pantomime. How many readers can honestly say that they weren't caught up in its magic too. Which of us didn't long to go through those cardboard shops and see what was inside, didn't want to pour that custard down the squire's trousers, didn't want to be part of that world of laughing, jolly, pretty, noble lovable people.

Do you remember your first visit to the pantomime? If it's a bit hazy, before you start this book, just turn to page fifty-two and read Sir Francis Burnand's recollections of a Boxing Night in 1842. It'll put you in just the right mood. You'll remember every detail and realise how very little its appeal has changed.

The first panto I saw, according to my Gran, was "Dick Whittington And His Cat". This obviously made a deep impression because, apparently, for the next five weeks I crawled around on all fours and refused to eat anything unless it was put down in a plate, on the floor. My Gran always said this was the moment she knew I'd go into show business.

My second panto stays with me because it was the first time I fell in love. Not with the principal girl (a very young Julie Andrews) but with the entire troupe of Terry Juveniles. I couldn't tell one from the other so it had to be them all. I remember being dragged away from the stage door of the London Casino, crying and screaming because I'd only seen ten of them come out—all with identical fringes and red cloaks.

Later on, of course, I got to thinking girls were soppy and it was then I fell in love with the real stuff of pantomime. I was about ten and watching that great slapstick comedian Lauri Lupino Lane convulsing a Christmas audience. I started crying and when asked why I replied "Oh, it must be the most marvellous thing in the world to make people laugh like that". This was the moment when I knew I'd go into show business. When I told Lauri this story he replied "That's right, go on, blame me!"

Although, as we see from this history, pantomime has undergone many violent and drastic changes, I think it basically remains the same. A glorious rag bag of flashy spectacle, leggy villagers, washer women with five o'clock shadows and three previous husbands ("The first one died, the second never did a day's work in his life and the third one went potty—that's one in the hole, one on the dole and one up the pole!"), popular songs, glorious slapstick and cleverly worked in speciality acts ("And for my third wish, Fairy Godmother, I'd like to hear Issy Bonn sing 'My Yiddisher Momma' "—"My child, your wish is granted"). All is acceptable in panto and when you read this fascinating story you'll realise it always was.

A good simple moral story with lots of laughs, a few frights and a bit of music seems always to have been the formula for entertaining the children. They never seem to have been overkeen on too much spectacle or too many love songs. How well today do we performers know the dreaded sound of seats going up and the patter of hundreds of tiny feet heading for the loo if the transformation scene should drag on or the duet grind on to an eighth verse and chorus.

Happily Mr. Wilson's book does not make us head for the exits. It is as entertaining and as full of fun as the subject he writes about. His enthusiasm for, and delight in, the pantomime comes through on every page. We've long been waiting for a concise and correct history of this peculiarly British entertainment and "The Story of Pantomime" is these things too.

As in almost any history of things theatrical, one or two performers seem to stand out head and shoulders above the rest. The two great pantomime names were, of course, 'Joey' Grimaldi and Dan Leno. Contrary to general belief I never actually saw them, but Mr. Wilson's descriptions of Grimaldi's tricks and business and of the immortal Leno's eccentricities make them both spring vividly to life. How strange that after the deaths of these two great innovators, sixty-seven years apart, pantomime fell into a sort of decline. What giants they must have been. Many of their original routines are still in use today. Grimaldi's soldier sketch and Leno's "Tree Of Truth" are just a couple I saw only last season.

Incidentally, Dan Leno, during the last fatal years of his illness, spent quite some time in a private hospital in Streatham. The hospital has long since disappeared and in its place is a children's playground, "The Agnes Riley Gardens". I like to think that the spirit of Dan, who made so many children happy at Drury Lane, is perhaps around there somewhere watching the kids enjoying themselves still.

I really believe pantomime should be a children's entertainment and like Mr. Wilson I tremble at some of the educational and moralising 1840 spectacles. We get great chunks of these in the book and fascinating they are too.

How relieved I was to discover that the hero hasn't always been a girl. I've never really understood why they should be and as a child I always found the fight scenes and heroics totally unbelievable when performed by a lady in "drag". The modern (and ancient) idea of men playing men's parts seems much more acceptable. I've worked with several male principal boys and did the kids love 'em. Edmund Hockridge tackled his fight scenes with such enthusiasm (roared on by the children) that one night he nearly cleaved the villain in two—and with a wooden sword! Peter Noone and Frank Ifield were two Dick Whittingtons the kids believed in absolutely, and they were both completely different. Peter made our hero a shy awkward boy up from the country while Frank made him a no-nonsense opportunist, but they both loved Alice Fitzwarren and their love songs were totally acceptable. Even today's sophisticated youngsters start shuffling about when a *girl* sings to a *girl* "You Made Me Love You".

After reading Mr. Wilson's graphic reconstructions of The Harlequinade we must all regret its passing. It sounds just the stuff to get the kids going and I have to grudgingly admit we have nothing like it at all in modern panto.

We do still have some marvellous "dames" though. Billy Dainty's homely, wild-limbed Mum and Terry Scott's "cod" regal creation are my own two favourites.

Mercifully, unlike so many chroniclers of theatre past, Mr. Wilson finishes on a highly optimistic note regarding the future of pantomime. Rightly so. In recent years more and more are being produced *and* are making money. Very important. A good panto is still the most expensive sort of show to mount and as long as it pays its way everyone is happy and we "pros" will always have the chance of taking part in our own very favourite entertainment.

Believe me, to be in the wings, with your heart thumping away in your throat, waiting for your first entrance on a Boxing Day matinee, is still the ultimate show business "trip". "Is it worth it?" you think, as your mouth gets drier and your hands get wetter, "I could have been at home with the mince pies and Guinness". Too late. "Where is that boy?" . . . "Here he comes now" . . . music, and suddenly you're out there. "Hello kids" you manage to say. "HELLO SIMON/JACK/BUTTONS/ROY" the roar comes back. You relax. "Yes" . . . "No!" . . . "Don't sit down!" . . . "Boo!" . . ."Hurray!" . . . "Look out he's behind you!". Yes everything is alright. The children *haven't* changed.

Dear Jocy, dear Dan, it's Christmas and "Here we are again!"

I

Our First Pantomime

IT was the chance discovery of an article in an old volume
of *Household Words* when it was under the editorship of
Charles Dickens that led me to ruminate once more upon
the fascinating subject of Christmas Pantomime and the
many changes it has undergone – while obstinately remain-
ing in essence and spirit more or less the same thing – since
it became established as one of the most characteristic and
typical of our national institutions.

The article begins with a forthright statement: "We take
it for granted," it says, "that every reader of *Household
Words* has a due respect for pantomime." Therein I think
I detect the voice of Dickens himself. It proceeds, with
loving and appreciative phrase in which at least the spirit
of Dickens, (who masterfully moulded all his contributors
into a unity of sentiment), is strikingly evident, to describe
pantomime as it was in the days of George the Second.

What the writer actually evokes is a performance of
Harlequin Sorcerer in 1753 and we are told that the scenery
and contrivances were "inimitable" and that the music was
almost entirely by Mr. Arne who himself played upon the
harpsichord!

Then follows a closely detailed description of the action
in which the chief characters are those of Harlequin, the
lover, Columbine whom he dauntlessly pursues through a
series of comical and exciting adventures, and Pantaloon,
her guardian and the ancient dupe and victim of many
pranks. Not a word, though, about Clown as a character.
But there *is* mention of Pantaloon's servant, the role which
later on the great Grimaldi was to develop into the leading
figure in pantomime.

And having thus evoked the eighteenth century entertainment the writer concludes: "We have seen a pantomime of our ancestors and our prevailing impression is that, with a few differences of detail, it is in the main very like the same description of a performance in the present year (i.e. 1853). There is not quite so much uproarious fun and we miss the spoken humour of the modern Clown, many of whose vagaries appear to be the peculiar property of the Harlequin. We note few gymnastic feats and mark the absence of 'hits' at the passing follies of the day."

Then comes his concluding speculative note. "Some of these days", the writer meditates, "we shall be gathered to the dead. Will any of our descendants in the year 1953 make a spiritual journey backwards to see any one of the pantomimes of the present year of grace? Let our pantomime writers and actors, our mechanists and scene-painters plume themselves with the thought of that possibility. Such things may be."

What true pantomime-lover could resist so tempting a challenge?

Leigh Hunt, in one of his most delightful essays, wrote: "He that says he does not like a pantomime, either says what he does not think, or is not so wise as he fancies himself. He should grow young again and get wiser."

That was written over a hundred years ago, but the words are as wise now as when Leigh Hunt, a great lover of pantomime first set them down.

But really, can you imagine anyone *not* liking a pantomime?

I think every playgoer must lovingly remember his first pantomime as one of the most important and exciting events of his life. For, you know, such a thing as a first pantomime, however lucky you may be, happens only once in a lifetime. And though, if you happen to be particularly young at the time, you may not understand all that is going on and there may be moments when some of the more grown-up part of the show causes you to fidget in your seat and incur the displeasure of your parents or whoever has been kind enough to take you, I am sure that on the whole the visit to that pantomime will linger in your mind for ever after as marking one of the red-letter days of your life.

Little scraps and glimpses, dim pictures of what you saw – of pretty Cinderella maybe, or of Dick Whittington, of the wonderful coach all lit up, of a comical cat, of a Fairy Queen or a comedian, of flying fairies and so on – will now and again come to you to remind you of a glorious occasion.

I know I shall never forget the time when I saw my first pantomime, though I should be ashamed to say exactly how long ago that was.

I was hardly five years old then, and it was in the days so long ago when London was a very different kind of city from what it is at present. There were no electric trams, no tubes, no motor-buses or cars of any kind. The buses were all horse-drawn and the streets were filled with horse traffic. Instead of taxis there were "hansom cabs", a ride in which was a great treat. The "clop-clop" of the horses made a very cheery sound.

The streets were narrower, too, and at night they were lit mostly by gaslight. Most of the shops kept open until a very late hour, and as the shop windows illuminated the thoroughfares it was quite easy to find your way about.

Of course, there was no such thing as radio and the cinema was unknown, for anything in the way of films had hardly got beyond the experimental stage.

Consequently the most popular form of entertainment was the theatre, and at Christmas-time it was possible to choose between many different performances in London. In fact, there was hardly a city or town or any place in the kingdom that could boast of a theatre that did not stage a pantomime.

Many of the London theatres in the West End and also in the outer districts were particularly noted for their pantomimes. Among them were Covent Garden, the Surrey Theatre, which was on the south side of the Thames, near Blackfriars Bridge; the Britannia Theatre, Hoxton, and the

Grand Theatre, Islington, both in North London; the Standard Theatre, Shoreditch, and the Pavilion Theatre, Mile End, which were on the eastern side of the city.

But the best pantomimes of all were to be seen at Drury Lane Theatre, and that, I am sure, was the place to which any boy or girl who knew anything about pantomime yearned to be taken at Christmas-time.

It was there that I was lucky enough to see my first pantomime, and two of the most amusing funmakers in it were Dan Leno and Herbert Campbell.

Perhaps the glamour of these names is dimming now, but any grey-haired relative, I am sure, will tell you that they were two of the most comical actors who ever amused the grown-ups as well as the children.

Dan Leno was a small, thin and active little man with a friendly but sad-looking face, and his arched eyebrows always gave him an expression of surprise and wonder. His companion, Herbert Campbell, was a jolly-faced fellow, big, heavily built and slow-moving. In perfect contrast they made the most felicitous partnership in the annals of Christmas entertainment. They were great friends and they appeared together in the Drury Lane pantomimes from 1888 until 1903.

Very often Dan Leno would be one of those comic, red-nosed and oddly-dressed women who, in pantomime, are always known as "dames". Sometimes he would be Aladdin's mother or Mother Goose or even a queen, while Herbert Campbell might be a king or a bold, bad robber. But whatever they were, in whatever guise they appeared, and in singing, playing pranks or dancing together they were a joy to watch.

As I was so young at the time and as it happened so long ago, I can't say I can remember much about *The Babes in the Wood*, the pantomime in which I saw this inspired couple. What I can recall is that Herbert Campbell was one of the Babes. Can you imagine how droll it was to see this big, good-natured fellow dressed in a velvet knickerbocker

"Little Lord Fauntleroy" suit, with a lace collar, and wearing a sailor's straw hat, sucking a great sugar stick and seated in a perambulator with his equally big baby sister? Dan Leno was the governess whose difficult duty it was to look after this troublesome couple of very naughty youngsters. It was nothing like so big a part as those he played in later pantomimes, but he made so much of it that it set him on the road to pantomime fame.

I can remember that part of the pantomime and also the part in which, when the Babes were lost in the wood and went to sleep under a spreading tree, gigantic birds flew down and covered them with equally gigantic leaves. I have forgotten all the rest of it, but I can still recall the impression, the magic and wonder of the changing scenes, the gay dresses, the flying fairies and the brilliant lights and the sparkle of the stage that seemed so far away, a fascinating glimpse of Fairyland seen from high up in the crowded theatre, where the scent of the oranges was very strong, for every child seemed to be engaged in eating one.

Stay! I do remember something else about that pantomime. It was the Harlequinade in which for the children the best of all the fun came in. It was in the Harlequinade at the end of the show that Joey the Clown played all his pranks, along with the aged Pantaloon, the Swell, the Policeman and the shopkeepers, while all the time the gay and spangled Harlequin skipped about the stage with his fairylike companion Columbine.

But there, what does the modern child know about the Harlequinade which was once the best part of that changing kind of thing we know as pantomime? Very little, I expect.

So before I come to more recent times I shall have to tell you something about the history and development of British pantomime, which has been an institution in this country for two hundred years. But don't be afraid and please don't shut the book just because I mention the unpleasant word "history". The history of pantomime in this country is full of fascinating stories about interesting people, about fairies and fairy-tales, about fun-making, about kings and queens, the princes and princesses and other heroes and heroines of nursery lore, about the people who devoted their lives to entertaining us every Christmastide.

2

How Pantomime Began

I EXPECT most of those who read this book know what present day pantomime is – a jolly sort of entertainment built around one of the favourite fairy-tales and nursery legends. It may be *Cinderella, Dick Whittington, Aladdin, The Babes in the Wood, Mother Goose* or *The Sleeping Beauty*, but whatever the subject it comes very much to the same thing. You are sure to have the comedians who make you laugh with their funny antics, the Principal Boy and the Principal Girl who, as hero and heroine, do the love-making and most of the singing, the Fairy Queen who performs wonders with her magic wand and sees that virtue is always rightly rewarded in the end, the ballet dancers, the jokes, the chorus songs and no end of pretty scenes and gay dresses.

Pantomime has been that kind of thing for many years, but it has undergone many changes and developments since it was first established in this country over two hundred years ago. I very much doubt, if it were possible for some survivor of the eighteenth century to visit one of our theatres during the Christmas season, whether he would recognise what he saw as pantomime.

If you look into the *Encyclopædia Britannica* you will find that the word pantomime is defined as "a dramatic entertainment in which the action is carried on with the help of special music and dancing, in which the performance or its adjuncts is conducted by certain conventional characters derived from the Italian 'masked comedy' ".

Well, that doesn't help us very much, does it? But it is quite a good description of what pantomime was when it was first introduced into England. As you may guess, it was not exactly the sort of entertainment designed for the amusement of the younger folk. It was rather like what we in these days would call mimed ballet.

The word "pantomime" is, in fact, of Greek origin and means "an imitator of things". "Pantomime", therefore, was originally the performer himself and not the play in which he appeared. He was what we should call a "dumb-show performer", who used no words, but indicated everything by his actions, gestures and movements.

Dumb-show acting accompanied by music goes a long way back in the history of the world. It is said to have been known among the early Chinese, Persians, Jews and Egyptians, and it exists among some savage tribes to this day as part of the merrymaking associated with holidays and feasts.

More than three hundred years before the Christian era it is said that the Greeks had a form of pantomime in which the performers danced to the accompaniment of music. This kind of performance found its way to Rome, and it became very popular with the Roman public, who were fond of being amused. The Emperor Augustus was a great encourager of these entertainments, and it is even said that another Roman emperor was so fond of pantomime that he appeared in such shows himself. They were not always strictly proper and, in the matter of undress, appear to have outdone some of our modern revues.

As Christianity grew in the Roman empire the pantomime declined and finally it vanished. A somewhat similar kind of entertainment, however, developed in Italy during the fifteenth century. In one play of the kind the characters of Arlecchino (or Harlequin) and of Punchello (or Clown) were introduced. Both were robust, comic characters who engaged in rough, knockabout fun.

Then to this kind of play were added some other characters who imitated or made fun of the various types of people in the Italian country districts. Just as we enjoy jokes about the supposed meanness of the Scots folk or the homeliness of the Yorkshire people, the Italians laughed over the characteristics of these provincial types.

Among the new characters were Pantaleone (or Pantaloon), a Venetian merchant; Dottore, a Bolognese physician; Spaviento, a Neapolitan boaster; Gingurto and Coviello, simple-minded boobies of Calabria; Gelsomino, a Roman dandy, and Beltramo, a Milanese simpleton.

But it was Arlecchino, a clumsy servant, who was the principal character. He was a cunning fellow who, despite his clumsiness, made mistakes, cheated and played practical jokes on his companions. He was not a graceful, dancing figure such as he later became in these plays.

The plays and the companies that performed them were known as the *Commedia dell'Arte*. During the reign of the French King Henry IV (1551–1610) a company visited Paris. At that time Arlecchino wore a costume consisting of a jacket, open in the front and fastened with ribbons, and tight breeches covered with patches of various coloured cloths. He had a straight black beard and wore a black mask, a slashed cap, a leather waistbelt, and carried a flat wooden sword. Now if you look at a picture of Harlequin as he used to appear in our pantomime Harlequinades you will recognise some of these features.

When Harlequin was introduced into England he was the principal character of the show, and that is why, so long after his importance had declined in favour of Clown, the old-fashioned pantomime of the eighteenth and nineteenth century always included his name. Thus it was, even to the time I can remember in my childhood, that the title was generally *Harlequin Puss in Boots*, or *Harlequin Dick Whittington* and so on.

Not all the characters of these Italian plays were introduced into England along with Harlequin. But the Neapolitan figure of Punchello or Policinello, or some similar name by which he was known, came to us in quite another form of entertainment. He was the origin of our dear old friend Punch, of Punch and Judy fame.

In the Italian shows the characters at the time used to improvise the dialogue as they went along. Later on the words were written down and learnt by heart. All sorts of plays were performed, but generally one story was much the same as another. It generally went like this:

Pantaloon is a jealous old man with a pretty daughter or ward, Columbine, whom he jealously protects against the artful plans of Harlequin, of whom he does not approve because he is a reckless, gay and penniless fellow.

Pantaloon will not consent to the marriage of Columbine with Harlequin, who thereupon makes up his mind to run off with the young lady. In order to make matters easy Harlequin bribes Pantaloon's servant (Clown) to help in Columbine's escape from her home. So when Harlequin is helping Columbine to escape through the window Clown throws himself into his master's way and so prevents him from stopping the young people. Then begins the old man's chase of the runaways whom he is never able to catch because Clown, though pretending to help him, constantly plays cruel tricks and puts him on to the wrong scent.

And there you have the simple story which was the origin of the Harlequinade. The Harlequinade was the most popular part of the pantomime as it was known in the early part of last century until it was gradually reduced and finally disappeared entirely in favour of the fuller development of the fairy-story.

It is said that the character of Harlequin appeared on the stage during the reign of Charles II. Certainly after the Restoration period the Italian characters were popular in many plays. An amusing piece entitled *The Emperor of the Moon* appeared in 1687 and, we read, "Harlequin and Scaramouch both appear and play off many tricks". There was much singing and dancing in the play and plenty of opportunity for pretty scenery and comical antics. But though Harlequin appeared in this and several later plays of the kind they were not described as pantomime.

3
England's First Pantomime

NOW this brings me to the important question: What was the first pantomime and who invented it?

Some authorities say that it was John Weaver, a Shrewsbury dancing master, who, in 1702, produced at Drury Lane Theatre a play entitled *The Cheats; or, the Tavern Bilkers*. It was described as "an entertainment of dancing, action and motion only" and the story was performed "by a selection of characters from the Italian comedy". According to all accounts it was not much of a success, but it created a taste for that kind of entertainment.

It was actually the actor John Rich who first described a play as pantomime. He was the inventor of the Harlequinade and he was the first to introduce the magical tricks and changes that became so popular. Besides this he was a clever performer as Harlequin, which he played in dumb-show, and he was the founder, too, of Covent Garden Theatre, which for so long was one of the principal homes of pantomime.

Rich, who was born in 1692, was the son of a lawyer who was a part-owner of Drury Lane Theatre. It is said that, as his education had been neglected and that as he had an impediment, he spoke very badly. He was evidently not cut out to be a successful actor, but he was excellent in performing silent parts and he was a good judge of acting as well as being the inventor of a particular kind of play. When his father died he became a manager with his brother of Lincoln's Inn Fields Theatre, which once stood on the site now occupied by the Soane Museum.

At first his company of players was so poor that he was forced to introduce some new kind of entertainment to attract the people. He called it pantomime. One of his first shows of the kind was called *Harlequin Sorcerer*, but though the title sounds rather attractive I don't suppose you would have greatly enjoyed sitting it all the way through. In any case, of course, it was invented for the benefit of the grown-ups, for I don't think that in those days it was the custom to take the younger people to the theatre. There was music and dancing in it and some of it at least was probably quite entertaining.

Part of it was composed of a story drawn from the Latin classics, but in between the acts came the kind of fun that might have amused the younger folk, for we read that another story was introduced concerning "the courtship of Harlequin and Columbine, with a variety of surprising adventures and tricks that were produced by the magic wand of Harlequin, such as the sudden transformation of palaces and temples to huts and cottages, of men and women into wheelbarrows and joint stools, of trees turned to houses, of colonnades to beds of tulips and mechanics' shops into serpents and ostriches".

From that time pantomime became the rage and Rich went on producing them, not at Christmastide – for that was a later custom – but at all times of the year. In one pantomime he introduced a troupe of performing dogs. His theatre was crowded every night and of all his pantomimes produced between 1717 and 1761 scarcely one was a failure.

As a result, David Garrick, much against his will, for he preferred to produce only serious plays, was forced to produce pantomime at Drury Lane Theatre, and there was great rivalry between him and Rich. In his pantomimes Garrick turned the silent character of Harlequin into a speaking character because he had no actor who could express himself so well in dumb-show as did Rich.

One of Rich's favourite tricks was to pretend that Harlequin was hatched from an egg. It was a famous piece of acting. As one writer says: "From the chipping of the egg, his discovery of motion, his feeling of the ground, his standing upright, his quick Harlequin trip round the empty shell – every limb, it is said, had its tongue, every motion its voice."

When he appeared as Harlequin, Rich wore a costume consisting of a loosely-fitting jacket and trousers made up of patches of various colours. It was not the sort of Harlequin presented in Victorian pantomime, but of the kind pictured by Watteau.

Most of Rich's pantomimes followed the familiar story invented by the Italians. Generally they began with Columbine running away from Pantaloon's house. Pantaloon would take up the pursuit and Harlequin would use his magical powers to defeat him. In this, of course, he was helped by Clown.

Harlequin, you must know, had a fortunate but rather unfair advantage over his enemies. His magic sword or bat was supposed to have the power of changing copper into gold, of cutting people in half and enabling Harlequin to jump through stone walls and leap over the tops of houses. Those coloured patches on his dress had a special meaning. The yellow stood for jealousy, blue for truth, scarlet for love, and black for invisibility. In striking his attitudes Harlequin always pointed to one or other of these colours.

All sorts of magical tricks and changes formed part of these pantomimes. Flying cars and mechanical monsters were introduced and some of the scenery was quite gorgeous and elaborate. The art of painting beautiful scenery for the stage owed a great deal to Rich, who employed people who had designed scenery for the Italian theatres. Up to his time the scenery used had been very simple.

But you must remember that in spite of the fun these pantomimes bore little resemblance to the kind of entertainment we know as pantomime. However, things began to shape that way in 1789 when *Robinson Crusoe* appeared for the first time as a play. Into the story the characters of Clown, Pantaloon, Harlequin and Columbine were introduced, and when Robinson Crusoe ended his adventures on the island Harlequin began his usual tricks and magical changes.

Pantomime was so popular at this period that many people, tiring of some of the subjects so often used, suggested that it was time that the writers of them should turn their attention to children's story-books and use some of the tales for stage performance. One writer suggested as a likely story *The Babes in the Wood*. "It would be vastly pretty," he said, "to see the pasteboard robin redbreasts let down by wires to cover the poor innocents with paper leaves." He also suggested that the public would be pleased to see the wolf and Little Red Riding Hood or Puss in Boots on the stage. But it was some years before this good advice was adopted by the pantomime writers.

4

Joseph Grimaldi, Greatest of Clowns

SOME may have wondered why Clowns are generally known as "Joey". They owe that to the name of Joseph Grimaldi, the greatest of all Clowns and probably the most popular artist who has ever adorned our English pantomime. He was a lovable and attractive person and I think we can rightly look upon him as one of the immortal figures of the stage. Many great writers have paid their tribute to him, among them Charles Dickens, who wrote the story of his life.

Joseph Grimaldi was born on December 18, 1778. His father, Giuseppe Grimaldi, was an Italian actor and ballet dancer who came to England to earn his living. His first appearance in London was as Pantaloon in *Orpheus and Eurydice* at Covent Garden Theatre, in February 1759. When he appeared later in a ballet at Drury Lane Theatre one writer said: "Grimaldi is a man of great strength and agility, he indeed treads the air. . . . If he has any fault he is rather too comical."

His first appearance in real pantomime was in *Fortunatus*, in which he played the part of Harlequin. Clown at that time, you must remember, was not an important character. In the summer Grimaldi went to Sadler's Wells Theatre (which was on the site of the present theatre of that name) to play in pantomime, for, as I have already said, it was not then confined to Christmas. He appeared as Clown, but he did not make it a particularly comical character, though it was the principal part of the show.

Born into the profession, it was inevitable that little Joe

should follow his father's profession. He was carried on to the stage when quite a baby, and when he was only four or five years of age he would stand at the side of the stage watching his father's antics. As he grew older he often played small parts such as imps and animals in his father's pantomimes, and on one occasion he acted with him as a miniature Clown made up exactly like his father.

Joe had a very early experience of the pains and penalties of clowning. His father was a very stern taskmaster and often thrashed him and treated him harshly. When he was only two he had a narrow escape from death. He was dressed as a monkey and, attached to a chain, was whirled round and round violently by his father. One night the chain broke and Joe was hurled into the arms of a man in the pit.

On another occasion, when he was only four years old, he fell through a trap-door to a distance of forty feet. It was a wonderful escape, but, as someone once wrote, little Joe must have had as many lives as a cat.

He was only eight when his father died. Not long before that happened the eccentric old man shammed death in order to test the affections of his two sons. One day he told the servant to inform the boys as soon as they had returned from a rehearsal that he had suddenly died. First of all they were to be brought into a darkened room, where he lay beneath a sheet, so that he might hear how they bore the news.

Little Joe, suspecting a trick, cried loudly, but his brother danced and sang with delight at the prospect of being free from a tyrannical father. Up sprang old Grimaldi and gave the undutiful son a severe thrashing, but the more artful Joe was petted and rewarded for his sham display of grief.

After his father's death Joe, although so young, had to work very hard. Every morning he had to walk from his home to the Sadler's Wells Theatre for a rehearsal. After dinner he had to walk to the theatre again, and there he worked from six until eleven o'clock, after which he had to walk home.

Sometimes he performed both at Sadler's Wells and Drury Lane on the same night. On one occasion he was so pressed for time that he ran from one theatre to the other in eight minutes. Another time he ran all the way from Sadler's Wells to the Theatre Royal, Haymarket, in fourteen minutes and, after playing a small part, ran back to Sadler's Wells in order to play Clown.

He was only three when he appeared in *Robinson Crusoe* at Drury Lane, but although he had begun his career so early and worked so hard it was some time before he found the opportunity to express his comic gifts in the part of Clown which he afterwards made so popular and famous.

His first big chance came in 1800, when he played in *Harlequin Amulet; or, The Magic of Mona*, at Drury Lane. In the first part he appeared as Punch, changing afterwards to Clown. It was a great success, but it meant very hard work for him. Punch's costume was so heavy and clumsy that it was more than he could bear during the whole of the entertainment. He had to wear a large and heavy hump on his chest and back, a high sugar-loaf hat, a long-nosed mask and heavy wooden shoes. The weight of the whole dress was enormous, and so it was a great relief to change into Clown's costume at the end of the sixth scene.

Grimaldi did not dress the part of Clown in the fashion by which we have known the character. Nor did he whiten and paint his face in the manner adopted by later Clowns. But he painted some red patches on his cheeks, so as to give the idea of a greedy boy who had smeared his face with jam in robbing his mother's pantry.

There was at least one other notable thing about this pantomime. There was a complete change in the style of Harlequin's dress. Up to this time the character had been played in the loose-fitting kind of costume I have already described. It was an actor named James Byrne who altered this in *Harlequin Amulet*. He invented a new idea for the dress. It is such as you have often seen pictured – a tight-fitting costume of gaily-coloured patches all covered with glittering metal spangles. In this he appeared as a very lively and striking figure, jumping and leaping in the most active way. No wonder he was a great success, but for all this spangled beauty he could not outshine the comic glory of Grimaldi's Clown.

But Joe Grimaldi's greatest triumph was yet to come. It was his appearance as Clown in *Mother Goose* at Covent Garden Theatre on December 26, 1806, that put him in the very forefront of comic entertainers – a place which he kept until the end of his brief career.

The kind of pantomimes in which Grimaldi appeared had changed considerably in style since the days of John Rich.

For one thing they did not supply the whole of the evening's entertainment. They were only very slight affairs performed after the principal play of the evening. In those days audiences expected a good deal for their money and before the pantomime came on it was customary to perform a serious play, very often one by Shakespeare.

The pantomimes were made up of a thin sort of story, a little fun and a number of songs, choruses and dances before Clown and Harlequin and their companions appeared on the scene and whiled away the rest of the time with fun and magical transformations.

Mother Goose or, to give it its full title, *Harlequin and Mother Goose; or, The Golden Egg*, was performed after the popular drama *George Barnwell*. Here is a brief outline of the story it unfolded:

Avaro, the miserly guardian of Colinette, breaks a promise made to Colin that he should marry his ward, in favour of the rich and ugly Squire Bugle, a part acted by Grimaldi. When the play opens the villagers are assembled to join in the preparations for the marriage and they sing:

Neighbours, we're met on a very merry morning,
  Lads and lasses dressed in all their bright so gay,
To celebrate the happy hour when, maiden shyness scorning,
  Sweet Colinette is married to the Squire today.

Old and young
Join in the throng,
Cutting nimble capers;
Haste to the church,
In the lurch
Leave care and vapours.
No one so sad
Hey! go mad,
Man and maiden seem to say:
If I know who
Prove but true,
Commenced may be my wedding day.

The Squire hates Mother Goose (who makes her entry by descending from the skies mounted on a gander) and orders her to be ducked in the village pond as a witch. She is saved by Colin, and as a reward she gives him the goose that lays the golden eggs, so making him rich enough to marry Colinette.

The miserly Avaro orders Colin to kill the goose in order that he may get the store of golden eggs inside, but before that can be done Mother Goose, with her magic powers, changes the Squire into Clown and the miser into Pantaloon and dares them to catch the lovers, now changed into Harlequin and Columbine.

Then the real fun of hide-and-seek begins and is continued through many different scenes. When the lovers are tracked down to a country inn tables appear at the tap of the magic wand. No sooner are the pursuers seated than they rise to the ceiling, along with the furniture, and remain there while Harlequin and Columbine are comfortably eating below.

The chase is continued to Fleet Street, where the famous clock of St. Dunstan's (still to be seen) descends by magic for them to change places with the figures of the two men who strike the hours. While Clown and Pantaloon look on in wonder their hats are changed into bells which the images strike with their clubs. Then the scene changes to the pleasure gardens of Vauxhall, where Clown comically imitates the musicians by playing on a broomstick, a tin kettle and other domestic utensils and articles.

Finally, after much more fun and jokes of the kind, Mother Goose relents, the Squire joins the lovers' hands and everybody joins in singing:

> Yet patrons who deign to view
> The sports our scenes produce
> Accept our wish to pleasure you
> And laugh with Mother Goose.

There was no spoken dialogue in *Mother Goose*. Everything was explained by action or by exhibiting written signs. For instance, if a landlord wanted his rent he would hold up a card inscribed with the words: "I have come for the rent." The tenant would then hold up another card inscribed: "I have no money." Moreover, the characters changed their costumes quite openly in order to appear as the transformed people of the Harlequinade. So you see it was a simple form of entertainment.

Mother Goose, we read, owed its great success almost entirely to Grimaldi, for it was by no means an expensive sort of production. It earned more than £20,000 for Covent Garden Theatre, which was a great sum for those days. It was played again later on and when the theatre was burnt down in 1808 *Mother Goose* was successfully transferred to the Haymarket Theatre.

Joseph Grimaldi, of course, appeared as Clown in many other pantomimes, in one of which he made the song "Hot Codlins" (toffee apples) famous. This was a story in song form and it always gave the people in the gallery great delight to supply the missing words in the last line. The song began:

> A little old woman her living she got
> By selling hot codlins, hot, hot, hot.
> Now this little old woman who codlins sold,
> Though her codlins were hot she was very cold,
> So to keep herself warm she thought it no sin
> To fetch herself a quartern of –

Then the people in the gallery would joyously shout "gin" and Grimaldi would sing the chorus:

Ri-tol-id-dy, id-dy, id-dy
Ri-tol id-dy, ri-tol-lay.

There were endless verses to this song, each ending with a blank which the gallery filled up. It became the custom for Clowns who followed Grimaldi to introduce "Hot Codlins" into the part. The gallery would clamour for it, and no Clown would dare to refuse their demand. As far as I know the last time the song was sung in a pantomime was in March 1926, when George Lupino, one of the last of the old-style Clowns, who belonged to a famous pantomime family of which I shall be writing later, introduced it during the Harlequinade at the Theatre Royal, Birmingham. Grimaldi also made another song entitled "Tippetywitchet" famous, and long after he died Clown in the Harlequinade was always expected to sing it.

How can the enormous popularity of Grimaldi to which so many have supplied testimony be explained?

Though he sang his songs in the pantomime, it does not appear that he had a particularly melodious voice, nor, unlike some later Clowns, did he dance. But he was naturally a very funny man who bubbled over with good humour. Look at his picture, not as a Clown, but as he was in private life. You will see the pleasant, honest-looking face of a very good-natured man.

Unlike a lot of other Clowns who performed gymnastical antics on the stage, walked on barrels or danced on stilts, he was not an acrobat. But he was full of real fun and diverting ideas and he could assume the most comical expressions. "Whether he robbed a pieman, opened an oyster, rode a giant cart-horse, imitated a sweep, grasped a red-hot poker, devoured a pudding, picked a pocket, beat a watchman, sneezed, snuffed, washed or nursed a baby – in all this he was extravagantly natural," said one writer.

Another writer, who remembered his last appearance on

the stage, once said: "When he sang 'A oyster crossed in love' such touches of real pathos trembled through its grotesqueness as he sat in front of the footlights, between a cod's head and a huge oyster that opened and shut its shell in time to the music, that all the children were in tears."

One of his most entertaining tricks was to dress himself up in bizarre disguises made out of all sorts of curious odds and ends. In one pantomime he appeared as a soldier. His hat was composed of a lady's muff with a crumb brush sticking out of the top like a plume. His boots were a pair of coal scuttles and his sword was a poker. And he would construct the semblance of a human figure out of giant cabbages, turnips, carrots and sticks of celery.

Above all, Grimaldi was the inventor of most of the tricks and diversions that continued to enliven the good, old-fashioned Harlequinade long after he was gone.

All the kind of fun of which it was composed was invented by Grimaldi and was copied by scores of Clowns who came after him. Though it was simple foolery, mainly intended to entertain the young folk, it was enjoyed just as much by the elders.

It is wonderful to think of the pleasure he gave to many thousands of people during the time he adorned the stage. How many of them were aware that he often went through his performances to the ringing laughter of the audience while he was suffering great pain?

For this business of amusing the public with comic antics was very hard work. You must remember that poor Grimaldi began when he was very young indeed and that as a young man he was miserably rewarded, for stage folk in those days were not very well paid. In his day there were no comfortable cars to help him on his journeys and travelling entailed great hardships. He grew old before his time and suffered illness which he bore very bravely. Moreover, his private life was not very happy, for there were many misfortunes in his family. His only son, who might have had a happy and very successful career on the stage, neglected all his chances and dying prematurely after continuous bouts of dissipation was a cause of much grief to his father.

In consequence of infirmity Grimaldi had to leave the stage before he was fifty. He made his last appearance at Sadler's Wells Theatre on March 17, 1828, and on June 27 he said farewell to the public at Drury Lane Theatre. That was a very sad occasion, for he, the once lively and active Clown, had to be carried on to the stage in an armchair, a crippled man. The theatre was crowded to the ceiling, and many of those who saw him – among them those who had followed his career from his boyhood – were in tears.

Seated in his chair and in his Clown's dress, he went through one favourite scene from a pantomime. "Even in this distressing condition," wrote Charles Dickens, "he retained enough of his old humour to succeed in calling down repeated shouts of merriment and laughter."

Then, having changed into his ordinary dress, he spoke the farewell address which had been written for him by Tom Hood, the poet. It brought more tears to the eyes of his sympathetic hearers.

"Eight and forty years have passed over my head," he said, "but I am going down the hill of life as that older Joe – Joe Anderson. Like vaulting ambition, I have overleaped myself and pay the penalty in an advanced old age. It is four years since I jumped my last jump, filched my last oyster, boiled my last sausage and set in for retirement. . . .

"For the benevolence that brought you hither, ladies and gentlemen, my warmest and most grateful thanks, and believe that of all Joseph Grimaldi takes a double leave, with a farewell on his lips and a tear in his eyes. Farewell! That you may ever enjoy the greatest earthly good health is the sincere wish of your faithful and obliged servant. God bless you all!"

Grimaldi was an invalid for the rest of his life, but it is said that he was always cheerful and interested in pantomime affairs. Every evening his friends would carry him pick-a-back to a fireside, where he would amuse them with his old jokes and stories. He died at the age of 58 in 1837 and was buried in the grounds of St. James's Chapel, Pentonville, North London.

I have read no more touching tribute to him than this: "A really kindly heart, an even temper, combined with a most childlike simplicity of character, caused him to be universally beloved in private as he was admired in public, while the statement, found after death among his papers, that in the solitary hours of declining life he could not recollect one single instance in which he had intentionally wronged man, woman or child, may have well found a ready echo in the breast of every one who ever knew him."

5

The Harlequinade

FEW of the modern generation have had the good fortune to enjoy the fun of a Harlequinade and will be wondering therefore what it was all about. Let me try to describe it as I remember it, though I was born much too late to see it in the days of its perfection, when it formed the best part of the performance, at least as far as the younger people in the audience were concerned.

The scene of a Harlequinade in its later days was generally a street showing a long row of shops gaudily decorated. There would be a butcher's, a baker's, a greengrocer's, a fishmonger's, a chemist's and so on. I am afraid that Clown, as may already have been guessed, did not set a very good example of honesty and correct behaviour to the youngsters who laughed over his ridiculous antics and enjoyed the fun, for all the tradesmen who kept these shops were the victims of his heartless practical jokes. Poor old Pantaloon, who hobbled after Clown – for he was supposed to be a very old man – was also the butt of the naughty fellow. Clown would address him as "father" or "old 'un", and I always had the impression that they were father and son. I often felt very sorry indeed for Pantaloon, who had to take the blame for so many of Clown's misdeeds and was not so active in escaping from the policeman, who was also an important figure in the Harlequinade.

Clown would steal all sorts of articles from the shops, and he seemed particularly fond of geese, legs of mutton and strings of sausages. You will generally see him pictured with one or other of these goods sticking out of the capacious pockets of his baggy breeches. From the grocer's he would take a slab of butter with which he would artfully grease the doorstep. Then he would knock at the door like a mischievous boy and would step aside and hide with Pantaloon gleefully watching. Out would come the unsuspecting grocer and would immediately topple over. The policeman, quickly on the spot, would also come a cropper and Clown would make off to some other mischief.

He was particularly unfair when it came to dividing up the fish from the fishmonger's window. Seated on the ground, he would give Pantaloon one very small fish, saying: "Here's one for you, father", and, taking two large fish himself: "There's two for me", and so on. The policeman would reappear. Pantaloon would hobble off, and the policeman would replace him, unnoticed by Clown, who went on dividing the spoil in this dishonest fashion. There would follow a general scramble and a chase in which everyone joined, but somehow or other Clown always managed to escape.

Clown would perform many such tricks of pilfering and mischief. He would steal babies from prams and would rob and assault the "swell" and other innocent passers-by, his favourite weapon being a large red-hot poker.

All this sort of thing would be performed in dumb-show and there was never much talking. Sometimes Clown would put the policeman through a mangle and he would emerge as a large, flat shape at the other end. He would pop a dog into a machine and there would emerge a long string of sausages. In fact, there was no end to the kind of mischief in which he indulged. It was all very wrong of him, of course, but how the children would laugh – and most of the grown-ups, too.

All the while this went on there would be soft but lively music from the orchestra and glittering Harlequin and dainty Columbine would hover about. They were supposed to be invisible and Clown would never notice their presence. In any case, he was far too busily occupied with mischief to do so.

It was Harlequin's part to produce all the magical tricks

and changes that helped to add to the fun and the excitement. He would perform his magic with a slap of his bat. At his silent command one shop would change into another, to the confusion of the unfortunate tradesmen. At his bidding doors would revolve and shop fronts would collapse. One article would be changed into another. Someone would go to bed and the bed would be transformed into a horse trough. There would be thrilling chases in which Harlequin, followed by Clown, would dive through windows and clock faces. It was a glorious turmoil in which I often longed to join.

Long before I was born the Harlequinade was much more elaborate. It was the custom to introduce many topical hits and allusions to the social and political events of the day. In that way the Harlequinade bore some semblance to the later revue. Here is what one writer has recorded of a Drury Lane Harlequinade in 1840:

"Some baskets of fruit are changed into three tables elegantly covered with fruit and flowers. Clown is crammed into a giant gooseberry and Pantaloon into a great raspberry which are respectively labelled 'Gooseberry fool' and 'Raspberry jam'. Then Harlequin draws a magic circle within which everyone is forced to dance, even the fish on a fishmonger's tray joining in.

"A view of Trafalgar Square and the National Gallery follows the placards on the wall, affording material for verbal jokes. A touch of Harlequin's bat changes the Nelson monument, a load of ship's blocks becomes the ship Victory, out of which is taken a tiny sailor.

"Clown and Pantaloon take refuge in furnished lodgings, which progresses to bare walls at the touch of Harlequin's bat to the bewilderment of the two lodgers. Chair after chair slips through the wall or the floor, fire irons take their way by the chimney, candles whirl round when wanted to light a cigar, window curtains dissolve to nothing, sofas and tables take their departure, chimney ornaments fling themselves at Clown, and the huge looking-glass falls on his head with a fearful smash, leaving him standing in melancholy astonishment in the empty frame."

Another writer at a later date says:

"You might have heard the laughter miles off when Clown stole the sausages and tried to put the baby in his pocket, and wasn't it capital fun when the policeman tumbled over the butter-slide Clown had just made before the doorstep, and then got pelted with flour bags conveniently pilfered from an adjoining baker's? But the best fun of all was when on getting up to pursue the culprit the policeman's hat was stolen by Pantaloon and a rabbit pie produced from the interior, to the great mortification and disgrace of the owner. . . .

"All this time Harlequin kept dancing across the stage and did the most wonderful tricks, changing barrels of beer into corpulent aldermen and cat's meat carts into sausage machines by merely touching them with his magic wand, and just as we were wishing the pantomime would last all night the scene changed into a glittering vista of diamonds and coral branches and a red light burned up that seemed to make everything ten times as brilliant and beautiful as before and then the curtain fell and it was over."

6

"Here We Are Again!"

THE Harlequinade was the most important part of the pantomime in Grimaldi's time, but it was not introduced until the latter part of the entertainment, when what was called the "opening" was concluded. This "opening" consisted of some fairy-tale or nursery story in which generally the characters included the village boy and girl who were sweethearts, a mother or some old woman described as "dame", and a wicked baron or equally wicked village squire who persecuted the virtuous characters and was properly punished in the end. It was considered right that pantomime should inculcate a good moral lesson.

The "opening" was quite short, but I don't think many of the children paid much attention to it, for naturally they were all impatient for the Harlequinade to begin.

A kindly, industrious writer of early Victorian days, E. L. Blanchard, who, among other things, wrote more pantomimes in his time than any other man, once said:

"Boys born sixty years ago* had at least one source of delight which children of a later generation will never know. In the days of the past when we were taken to the theatre for our holiday-treat at Christmas the true hero of our imagination was Harlequin. . . . Harlequin would perform his feats of transformation continuously through a long series of adventures in which we were all greatly interested by a steady succession of surprises of the most astonishing kind; and as every trick had a sort of political or social significance a vast amount of information about passing events was concurrently imparted to the youthful spectator who was found abstractedly burying the little knuckles of his fists in

---

* That is to say about 1820—AUTHOR.

39

the folds of his chubby chin on each new attitude of the nimble wonder-worker."

And, of course, the same young spectators were interested in the frolics of Clown. Though they may have yawned during the "opening", they always knew what was sure to come. What they waited for so impatiently was the sudden appearance of the Fairy Queen, whose duty it always was to transform the characters into those of the Harlequinade. This gave rise to what was called the Transformation Scene, that spectacle of dazzling beauty on which the scene-painters lavished their art.

Waving her wand, the Fairy Queen would perform her magic as she recited some pretty rhymes.

For instance, in one pantomime based on the story of Guy Fawkes she exclaimed:

> Lovers stand forth. With you we will begin.
> You will be fair Columbine – you Harlequin.
>
> King Jamie there, the bonnie Scottish loon,
> Will be a famous cheild for Pantaloon.
>
> Though Guy Fawkes now is saved from rocks and axe,
> I think he should pay the powder-tax.
>
> His guyish plots blown up – nay, do not frown;
> You've always been a guy – now be a Clown.

In another Drury Lane pantomime the Fairy Queen's commands ran:

> Fair Alice, as this privilege is mine
> Appear at once as graceful Columbine.
>
> Our merry monarch shall tonight begin
> A new career as spangled Harlequin.
>
> As some crosses might your progress chafe,
> This wand shall through your wand'rings keep you safe.
>
> Now then antiquity demands his boon:
> Dame Durden, hence be tottering Pantaloon.
>
> I'll make this knight who much deserves our pity
> A witty antic – not an antic witty (antiquity).
>
> So as of old our Christmas revels crown
> A comic, capering, true Grimaldi Clown.

In Blanchard's *Hey Diddle Diddle* it was the Spirit of Love
who first spoke with:

> Be mine the task these lovers to unite:
> Hopeful, as Harlequin, give first delight.
> Whilst you, Rosa, you with him shall combine
> The charms of youth and grace as Columbine.

Common Sense then steps in with:

> But Common Sense knows, since the world began,
> The course of true love never smoothly ran;
> So rivalry once more shall step in,
> With one more Columbine and Harlequin.

Whereupon King Nonsense adds:

> And I, to gain a couple of buffoons,
> Provide a pair of Pantaloons.

Then says Common Sense:

> Justice must be done, to please the town,
> And will be best done with this change to Clown.

And finally King Nonsense steps in again with:

> On my domains you're poaching, Sense, my boy,
> I'll give you Clown in young Hobbledehoy.

Again we come upon this in *Valentine and Orson* at Covent
Garden Theatre in 1880:

> Farewell to Valentine and Orson. Soon
> You'll welcome Clown and dear old Pantaloon.
> No sooner said than done. And Eglantine
> Will be replaced by sparkling Columbine.
> To Harlequin our Valentine gives way;
> That's all you can expect from Pacolet,
> Except the magic master-mind, don't lose it,
> Of course you know exactly how to choose it
> In worthier keeping I could not bestow it,
> All I have got to say is – go it!

Fairy Prism uttered these lines in *Jack and the Beanstalk* at
Drury Lane in 1859:

> This is my realm and I need not delay
> The pantomime fun that's in your way.
> Jack shall as Harlequin at once appear
> And with his Rose as Columbine be near.
> Still in Giant's head are brains too soon
> May serve as those of doddling Pantaloon.
> Old Goody Greyshoes, add to your renown
> By reappearing as a merry Clown.

Here is yet another rhyme with which the Fairy Queen performed her magic:

> Before you go, one favour I must ask,
> Let me impose a little further task;
> This time of year – the children wise from school,
> Delight to see the big ones – play the fool.
> Time presses, so we will let the fun begin:
> Appear Clown, Columbine, Pantaloon and Harlequin.
> Now all being ready and expectation keen,
> We'll complete our transformation with a jolly scene.

Or, more simply still, the lines would run:

> Now let all change as suits the time of year,
> And all our old pantomimic friends appear.

Can you imagine what a thrilling moment that was when the change was made and all the old favourites appeared?

There would be dazzling lights of red and green from the sides of the stage and on would come Clown and his companions to the joy of the children.

In the earlier pantomimes the characters would change their costumes in full view of the audience. Most of them concealed their Harlequinade finery under outer clothing and their heads were hidden under big masks which could be quickly thrown off.

When Grimaldi first appeared as Clown he would cry: "Hullo, here we are again!", words which all good Clowns subsequently copied. That was the signal for the fun to begin and often it went on for ten or a dozen scenes.

"But what about that transformation scene?" I hear someone reminding me.

Ah! that in its time was something of real delight that

caused everyone to gasp with admiration and wonder. It was a glimpse of Fairyland in all its dazzling beauty.

It was that brilliant scene-painter William Beverley who first made the transformation scene so popular. In 1849 he painted some beautiful scenery for a fairy play called *The Island of Jewels*. In one scene the gradual dropping of the leaves of a giant palm tree disclosed a group of fairies supporting a large jewelled coronet. This was so much admired that the producers of the pantomime copied the idea and soon every pantomime had its gorgeous transformation scene.

How lovely they were. Sometimes in our modern pantomimes you see them still, though alas! they are no longer used as a background for the introduction of the Harlequinade.

Curtains, all glittering with tinselled jewels, would rise and fall. They would be transparent and through them you could get tantalising glimpses of the further wonders behind. Sometimes the scene would be "The Bower of Bliss", "The Realm of Delight", "The Silver Cascade of the Lily Bell Fairies in the Land of the Cloudless Skies", "The Valley of the Golden Sands", "The Floral Realms of the Kingdom of Fancy" or something equally remote and beautiful.

Gauze-winged fairies would hover in the air as the scene gradually changed. Giant sea-shells would open, disclosing within some lovely fairy reclining luxuriantly at her ease. Giant flowers of orchid-like beauty would expand to reveal more wonders. Everything glittered and sparkled, bathed in light that simply dazzled the eyes.

In 1860 the transformation scene in the Haymarket Theatre pantomime *Queen Ladybird* disclosed real fountains with jets of water shooting up into the air and glassy pools reflecting the gorgeous dresses of the fairies.

Yes, the transformation scene as earlier generations used to know it, was a glimpse of Fairyland just as children imagined it, only perhaps rather more wonderful and splendid.

7

Clowns and Harlequins

IT is true that the death of Grimaldi left a gap never after completely filled, but it would be a mistake to think that there never were any really funny Clowns after his day. The Harlequinade continued to be popular for fifty years or so after he had gone, and though no other Clown was ever such a great favourite there were many who became popular.

His greatest successor was Tom Matthews, who played Clown at Drury Lane Theatre for nearly forty years and did not leave the stage until 1865, after his appearance in *Hop o' My Thumb; or, Harlequin and the Seven-Leagued Boots*. He lived to be 84 and he died at Brighton in 1889. He learnt all the tricks of clowning from Grimaldi himself, whose favourite pupil he was at Sadler's Wells Theatre.

One of the last people to write about him was Sir Francis Burnand, who for many years was editor of *Punch*. He remembered seeing him as a child, and this is what he says about him in his autobiography.*

"He waddled about bow-legged, did no acrobatic tricks, never danced, was always pilfering in the most innocent manner possible, knocked frequently at shop doors, hiding himself twice but immediately after the third knock lying down in front of the threshold so as to ensure the tripping up of the incautious and irate tradesmen over his prostrate body, when he, the artful, comic, mischievous Clown, would slip into the shop and reappear with all sorts of stolen goods, hams and turkeys under his arm and sausages hanging out of his pockets, just in time to come into a violent collision with the now furious tradesmen, whom he

* Those who read this passage aloud are warned to take a very deep breath. —AUTHOR.

would incontinently floor with one of his own hams, and at the watchword 'Look out, Joey; here's a policeman coming' given by the faithful but weak-kneed ally old Pantaloon, he would rush off the stage and on again, followed by a mob, when, in the middle of a regular 'spill and pelt' while everybody appeared to be assaulting everybody else, he would somehow or another manage to escape the hands of several constables, as the scene changed and light and airy music ushered in the Harlequin, masked, with pretty Columbine to execute some graceful *pas de deux*."

Clowns generally acted as instructors to younger pupils, and so their business and the secret of their tricks were handed down from one generation to another.

One of Tom Matthews's pupils was Jeffreys, who called himself Jefferini, for it was a favourite notion of many Clowns to give themselves a foreign-sounding name. I suppose they thought it looked more important on the playbills. Jefferini was a tall man whose long legs made his leaps through doors and windows very dangerous. The children who so much enjoyed his comical antics little knew that, like poor Grimaldi, he often went through his performance suffering great pain.

The leaping and tumbling that Clown had to do was often very dangerous. When, for instance, Clown jumped through a shop window men stood behind ready to catch him. Sometimes, however, they were not there at the time – and they took care not to be unless properly bribed with beer-money – and then poor Clown suffered injury, though he had to hide the fact when he returned to the scene.

Another amusing Clown was Harry Boleno, whose real name was Mason. As a boy he went to school near Sadler's Wells Theatre, and his ambitions were stirred by frequent visits to the theatre, where he sometimes had a glimpse of Grimaldi. This inspired him to imitation and the resolve to be a Clown himself. When he left school he obtained employment at the theatre. Along with some other boys he had to jump up and down under painted canvas to imitate the action of waves. It was a very modest beginning to a stage career, but very soon he had his first big chance, for at Grimaldi's last performance in 1828 he appeared as a lemon when Clown mixed a bowl of punch.

When he grew older he obtained work in a circus and later on he was Clown at Drury Lane for eleven years. His last appearance was at the Surrey Theatre in 1874. He is described as a grave and rather peculiar-looking man whose appearance hardly suggested the rollicking humour which he displayed on the stage.

One very clever Clown who specialised in dancing was Flexmore, who died in 1860 at the early age of thirty-four, after an illness due to his hard work on the stage. He is described as "a Clown whose fun and frolic never cease, whose vaults, leaps, falls, dances and aerial flights kept alive to the very end". He is said to have been the most active Clown that ever delighted a pantomime audience.

He was the son of a dancer and as a boy worked in a warehouse during the day. But at nights he obtained work at music-halls and theatres in order to earn sufficient to support his mother. Though he became one of the most graceful of dancers, he was a young man before he learnt his first step.

His first appearance as Clown was at the Olympic, a theatre that has long since vanished. His talent was quickly recognised, and he was engaged to play in pantomime at the Princess's Theatre, another vanished theatre, which stood in Oxford Street and was a very popular home of Christmas entertainment. While he was there he added to his popularity by his clever imitations of famous ballet dancers. He learnt much about dancing from his wife, who was the daughter of Auriol, a French Clown.

It was Flexmore who invented the style of costume in which Clown was dressed right up to modern times. It was different from the kind of dress worn by Grimaldi and Tom Matthews. Grimaldi's costume was really an exaggeration of the ordinary dress worn in his day, or just a little before his time. In those days a smart young man wore a black wig brushed down the back and tied in a pigtail. Round his neck he wore a lace collar. His breeches were fastened below the knee and he wore silk stockings with embroidered "clocks" and bright-coloured shoes with a buckle or rosette.

In burlesquing this style Grimaldi turned up the wig at the back, wore a large ruffle instead of a lace collar and pulled the breeches above the knees so as to make them baggy and provide room for pockets big enough to hold the legs of mutton, geese and other stolen goods. He exaggerated the "clocks" on the stockings and the rosettes on the shoes and covered the costume with bright-coloured spots and patches.

Flexmore changed this style. Being a dancer and anxious to keep his legs free, he wore tights and short, frilled trunks embroidered with red and blue braid.

A playgoer who saw the pantomime *La Belle Alliance; or, Harlequin Humour and the Field of the Cloth of Gold* at Covent Garden Theatre in 1855 wrote this about Flexmore:

"The life and soul of the Harlequinade was Mr. Flexmore, who possesses quite as much humour as activity and during all his extravagant feats and unheard-of rascalities he never once loses sight of the character he assumes from the beginning. In short he *acts* the part as well as tumbles and grimaces it. Besides his well-known graphic imitations of opera dancers Mr. Flexmore performed sundry ingenious feats on a couple of wooden horses in capital mimicry of the exploits at Astley's." (Astley's, I should explain, was a popular place of circus entertainment.)

Another Clown who seems to have been very popular was Huline, of whom someone writing in 1852 said: "A more dexterous and nimble Clown was never seen. His performance on two chairs and four bottles was little short of wonderful; his scene with a dog almost as clever as himself, and which he had evidently trained, was remarkably diverting and his dance on stilts with a negress was quite as droll as it was difficult and dangerous. Mr. Huline dances a hornpipe in the most approved pantomimic style and possesses all the essential requisites of humour and activity, being a Clown of the first water now that Clowns must perforce be tumblers as well as thieves, wits as well as rogues, mischief-makers no less than victims of mischief – which was not the case in the days of Grimaldi."

There were many other Clowns who were popular during Boleno's time and later – short Clowns and tall Clowns, thin Clowns and fat Clowns, Clowns who were active and acrobatic, Clowns who introduced performing dogs, Clowns who were content to make you laugh with their jolly grin and their mischievous tricks at pilfering. There was even at one time a lady Clown, a Miss Cuthbert, who performed the part in *The Magic Mistletoe; or, Harlequin Humbug* at the Strand Theatre in 1856, but it seems that she was not a very great success.

I have even discovered records of a Harlequinade performed entirely by children. That happened in the pantomime *Robin Hood* at the Adelphi Theatre in 1878 and this is what one writer said of it:

"It is impossible not to envy the boys who have attained the summit of a young theatregoer's ambition in being allowed to play Clown. It is eminently children's pantomime and on the first performance the theatre was taken by storm by children. Juries of at least twelve, with the foreman and forewoman much larger and older than the rest, sat in several of the private boxes, and the gallery was filled with persons of tender age who were ready to assist Master Coote, the Clown, when he paused for a word in the time-honoured singing of 'Hot Codlins'. A boy who would address a grown-up Clown as 'Sir' pays apparently no respect to a merryman of his own age, but the interruptors were vanquished by the satire of Master Coote, who begged to be excused for observing that 'one fool is quite enough at a time'."

Several of the young people who appeared in this juvenile Harlequinade subsequently made a name for themselves as

From the Illustrated London News, 1876

HIS FIRST PANTOMIME: AN EARLY VICTORIAN STUDY

From the *Illustrated London News*

MAKING THE "PROPS": A PANTOMIME WORKSHOP IN 1870

grown-up artists, among them being Master Bert Coote, who became a well-known comedian, and Katie Seymour, who was a popular favourite at the Gaiety Theatre.

Most Clowns took to the business very early in life and many of them came from families associated with the theatre. If a Clown had a son it was as natural for him to become a Clown as for a daughter to become a Columbine. Families like the Bolognas, the Rowellas, the Deulins, the Lauris, the Paynes and the Lupinos gave any number of Clowns, Pantaloons, Harlequins and Columbines to the stage. The traditional business would be handed down by word of mouth from father to son and it is wonderful how in this way it was preserved.

Only a few years ago I met an old man whose last appearance as Clown was before the 1914 war. He had learnt the business from an uncle who had been Clown for many years at the Royal West London Theatre, once well-known for its pantomimes, but now forgotten. This uncle had learnt how to be a Clown from Tom Matthews, who, as I have previously told, was a pupil of the great Grimaldi.

There have been Clowns of all kinds and of the most varied accomplishments and many who enjoyed a long and success career in pantomime. But there cannot be many old actors left who in their time have played the part.

One great favourite who made the children laugh for many Christmases and who is still remembered by older playgoers was Harry Payne. He was the son of a well-known and clever pantomime actor who often performed with Grimaldi, and he began his stage career when very young by playing Harlequin. One evening in 1865 Clown fell ill and Payne took his part so successfully that he went on playing Clown, most at Drury Lane Theatre, for the rest of his life. He died in 1895.

Though he was never married, he was devoted to children. He had a particularly appealing way with them, and there are many stories of his little acts of kindness. Though Clowns used to play such cruel jokes on the stage they were

D

nearly always very kindly men in private, but few were so tender-hearted as Harry Payne.

He was followed at Drury Lane by George Lupino, whose family has been associated with pantomime for two hundred years. Then came Whimsical Walker, who was the last of the Drury Lane Clowns. He appeared there for twenty-five years, and in the last years of his life, when there was no longer any opportunity for him in pantomime he made an annual appearance at Olympia Circus, where the children were always delighted to see him. He died in 1934 at the age of 84.

Pantaloons were never such great favourites as Clowns, but there were several actors who were particularly successful in the drolleries of the doddering old fellow who shared Clown's mischief and generally received all the hard knocks.

James Barnes was probably the most celebrated among them and he first played the part in 1809 at the Lyceum Theatre. Of him an old playgoer once wrote: "As for old Barnes, the Pantaloon, he was unique and unsurpassable, the most perfect type imaginable of senile imbecility, receiving knocks and cuffs with placid resignation and tottering about as if he perpetually expected to be knocked down and set up again like a ninepin."

Then we come to famous Harlequins, a part which many notable actors played in their time. It was John Rich who first made the part popular with his graceful, lively movements and acting in dumb-show. After his time Harlequin was generally performed by a skilled dancer, for Clown has become much more important in the Harlequinade and won most of the glory.

James Byrne, who, according to Grimaldi, was the best Harlequin of his time, belonged to a dancing family, and was originally a member of the Drury Lane ballet. It was he who originally designed the glittering, multi-coloured, tight-fitting costume of the part. It was a very expensive affair. It was composed of over three hundred pieces of cloth sewn on to a silk foundation and was covered with thousands of metal spangles that sparkled wonderfully under stage lighting. According to one authority, there were 48,000 of them, weighing three pounds, on each Harlequin's dress, so as every Christmas scores of Harlequins frolicked in pantomime up and down the land millions of spangles must have been used.

John Bologna, jun., who so often played Harlequin in Grimaldi's Harlequinades, was also of Italian parentage, and made his first appearance as a circus performer. His son Jack was also a popular Harlequin.

Another famous Harlequin was Tom Ellar, who, in Grimaldi's time, was notable for his leaps and bounds and feats of agility. One of the feats he was called upon to perform was to fly (on wires, I suppose) from the back of the gallery to the far extremity of the stage – a perilous descent of more than 200 feet.

It is said that he had the curious art of spinning his head round like a teetotum, a trick which he learnt from old Bologna. Like so many members of his profession, who, in his day, were ill paid for their task of amusing the public, he died in poverty.

Many famous actors played the part during their time, among them Edmund Kean who, it is said, owed much of his suppleness to this early training in Harlequin agility.

Many well-known dancers, too, played the part of Columbine, but none of them attained the fame in the part that rewarded so many Clowns and Harlequins.

8

A Hundred Years Ago

BEFORE going on to describe the kind of pantomime that developed after Grimaldi's time, I would like to present a glimpse of the pantomime of a hundred years or so ago as it was seen by a small boy of the period.

This excellent description was written by Sir Francis Burnand, who, in his old age, recalled his first pantomime, which he saw at Drury Lane Theatre on Boxing Night, 1842. It was *Harlequin and William Tell; or, the Genius of the Ribston Pippin.*

First of all he pictures the exciting scene inside the crowded theatre before the rise of the curtain – the boys and girls in their best suits and dresses eagerly sucking oranges and eating sweets, but all impatient for the pantomime to begin; the sellers of ginger-beer and lemonade and such refreshments forcing their way between the seats of the pit and gallery. Then he continues:

"A sharp tap on his desk by the conductor of the orchestra calls everyone to order. In a second there is a hush, a silence. And then – oh glorious moment in the Christmas life of a town-bred child – the overture to the pantomime commences! What overture can ever equal a first-rate overture to a pantomime on the first night of performance? What drawings-in of breath, all of a quiver! Fine parts for the deep bass of the brass, splendid chances for bassoon, cymbals and drums of all sorts and sizes! Crash! bang! – the green curtain has long ago disappeared, showing the gay 'act-drop' behind it. And now after the final fortissimo, followed by deafening applause, the facing round of the conductor in order to bow his acknowledgments to the audience and, it may be, to finish up with 'God save the Queen' and *then* a great silence, the orchestra plays mysterious music and – oh joy, yet dread

and terror! – the curtain rises on some gloomy cave of fearful demons whose nearer acquaintance not a boy among us
under eight years of age would be eager to cultivate.

"Afterwards came the good fairies, the sprites, and before
ten o'clock we were roaring with laughter at Joey the
Clown and were joining the audience in the uproarious
demand for 'Hot Codlins', which song sent us all into con-
vulsions of laughter, especially when the Clown imitated
the little old woman (the heroine of the song) who, as was
related, was deposited 'on her latter – head?' asked the
simple Clown. 'No – end,' shouted the audience, knowingly
but rudely. Whereupon the Clown winked and, rejecting the
suggestion, went at once into the highly intelligent chorus,
which was, I fancy, 'Rum-ti-tiddy-iddytiddy-iddy', with
which everyone was so enraptured that nothing but its
treble encore would satisfy them.

"The whacking, the banging, the horse-play, the tom-
foolery of the 'comic scenes' of those ancient pantomimes!
Well, it certainly did delight the children: we gloried in the
Harlequin, loved the Columbine to desperation, loved the
Clown and were ready to bully and laugh at the poor old
doting Pantaloon. . . . Everything was over, blue and red
fire and all, by eleven, and we children went home to bed, so
very happy, but oh, so very tired."

Well, tastes have not changed so much in a hundred years
as far as simple fun is concerned, and I am sure the most
blasé modern child would have enjoyed that kind of entertainment just as much as did young Master Burnand over
a hundred years ago.

Another well-known writer has described a pantomime of
the same period. It is Thackeray, who adored pantomime all
his life. He wrote a fanciful description of an imaginary
performance of *Harlequin and the Fairy of the Spangled Pocket-
handkerchief; or, the Prince of the Enchanted Nose*, which you
may accept as the kind of pantomime which he had so often
seen. He says:

"Lives there a man with soul so dead, the being ever so

blasé and travel-worn, who does not feel some shock and thrill at that moment when the bell (the dear familiar bell of your youth) begins to tinkle and the curtain to rise, the large shoes and ankles, the flesh-coloured leggings, the crumpled knees, the gorgeous robes and masks finally of the actors ranged on the stage to shout the opening chorus?"

Perhaps I should explain that in these pantomimes of a century ago the characters in what was known as the "opening", or first part of the performance which was concerned with some fairy-story or legend, always wore huge masks which they afterwards threw off when, at the bidding of the Fairy Queen, they were transformed into the familiar characters of the Harlequinade.

Thackeray goes on to describe the story of the "opening" and he continues:

"Fairy Bandanna in her amaranthine car drawn by Paphian doves appeared and put a stop to the massacre. King Gorgibus became Pantaloon, the two giants first and second Clowns, and the Prince and Princess (who had been all the time of the Fairy's speech and actually while under their father's scimitar unhooking their dresses) became the most elegant Harlequin and Columbine that I have seen for many a long day . . . the music began a jig, and the two Clowns (after saying 'How are you?') went and knocked down Pantaloon."

What Thackeray says about "first and second Clowns" requires one more word of explanation. In time it became the custom to represent the Harlequinade with a double set of characters – two Clowns, two Pantaloons and so forth. They appeared in alternate scenes. Perhaps it was thought that by this means they would double the supply of fun, but many old pantomime-goers did not like the custom, which, they declared, was due to the fact that since the days of Grimaldi, Clowns had ceased to be so funny and were incapable of carrying on the Harlequinade by their single efforts. Nor did these old playgoers like the introduction of some new characters into the Harlequinade – the "sprites" who were just very active acrobats who tumbled about the stage while Clown and Pantaloon performed their old antics.

The pantomimes of this period were often based upon very odd subjects. It would be vastly interesting to have a glimpse of the pantomime that bore such a title as *Harlequin and the Tyrant of Gobblemupandshrunkthemdowno; or, the Doomed Princess of the Fairy Hall with Forty Blood-red Pillars.* That actually was the subject of one Christmas entertainment, and there were many others with equally strange labels.

I am afraid it was often thought that the pantomime should be the means of instructing the children as well as entertaining them.

Let me give you an example of one of these curious entertainments which contrived to mix up a lot of schoolroom instruction with the fun. It was *Little Jack Horner; or, Harlequin A.B.C. and the Enchanted Region of Nursery Rhymes,* and it was described as "an entirely Allegorical, Beautiful, Comical, Diverting, Educational, Fanciful, Gorgeous, Hyperbolical, Intellectual, Jovial, Keen, Laughable, Merry, Novel, Original, Peculiar, Quizzical, Romantic, Splendid, Transcendental, Unobjectionable, Volatile, Waggish, X-travagant, Youthful, and Zigzaggy" pantomime.

It sounds a rather forbidding kind of entertainment, doesn't it? A description of the opening scene hardly makes it seem more attractive. It began in "The dark mists of Ignorance", which showed a vast inkstand around which were grouped characters representing the schoolbooks of the period – the grammars and the arithmetics – and at the sides of the stage were crowded "wretchedly clad children with Tag-Rag and Bobtail as chiefs".

The character representing Intelligence announced his hostility to another character representing Ignorance and some sort of warfare began.

Before hostilities broke out, however, there was a ballet introducing the Letters of the Alphabet, who were children each bearing a large letter, and it was Intelligence who described them as they marched on:

A was an Archer who shot at a frog.
B was a Butcher who kept a big dog.
C was a Captain all covered with lace.
D was a Drunkard who had a red face.
E was an Earl with pride on his brow.
F was a Farmer who followed the plough.
G was a Gambler who had all but luck.
H was a Hunter who hunted the buck.
I was an Innkeeper fond of society.
J was a Judge of far-famed notoriety.
K was a King who once governed the land.
L was a Lady, who had a white hand.
M was a Miser who hoarded up gold.
N was a Nobleman gallant and bold.
O was an Oyster-maid with a black eye.
P was a Policeman who loved rabbit-pie.
Q was a Queen who was fond of egg flip.
R was a Robber who wanted a whip.
S was a Sailor who spent all he got.
T was a Tinker who mended a pot.
U was an Usher who had a great rod.
V was a Victim inclining to nod.
W was a Watchman grown crazy and old.
X was old Xerxes, a warrior bold.
Y was a Youth who in love cried "Heigho!"
Z was a Zany, our old friend Pierrot.

After a combat with such horrid enemies as the embodiments of the Multiplication Table, Wine and Spirit Measure, Apothecaries' Weight, Troy Weight, Long Measure, Dry Measure and Pothooks and Hangers, Little Jack Horner found himself in a scene showing "a vast field of observation, with the abodes of Science and Art in the distance", and Ignorance rushed on exclaiming:

What, out to flight? Must Ignorance lose the day?
Throw up some barriers in his way!
Let English Grammar pour its forces out –
He'll never know what Syntax is about.
Personal Pronouns – I, Thou, He, She, It,
We, You and They, just bother him a bit.
                    PERSONAL PRONOUNS *enter*.

Auxiliary Verbs, teach this aspiring buffer
What 'tis to be, to do and what to suffer.
                    AUXILIARY VERBS *enter.*
Arithmetic, let addings and subtractions
Perplex him with the vulgarest of fractions.
                    ARITHMETIC *enters.*
Geography, the wide world bring news of,
And your great globe just show the real use of.
                    GEOGRAPHY *appears.*
Come, Mathematics, with your rounds and squares,
Trip up this daring stripling unawares.
                    MATHEMATICS *enters.*
Whilst Algebra with X meaning dim
Keep the unknown quantities unknown to him.
                    ALGEBRA *enters.*

Jack, however, kept a stout heart, exclaiming:

In vain you raise new terrors – I despise them
And as for difficulties, Jack defies them.

I am glad to say that in the end he overcame all his enemies, to the discomfiture of Ignorance and the joy of Intelligence.

It may have been a pretty and amusing pantomime, but I am sure many of the young members of the audience must have felt at times that they were back in the schoolroom again.

But there were many more pantomimes of this peculiar kind, and some of them were written round quite melancholy themes, conveying moral lessons which, while no doubt very valuable in the eyes of teachers and instructors, could hardly have been the kind of fun that holiday-making children had the right to expect.

About *Little King Pippin and Harlequin Fortunatus and the Magic Purse and Wishing Cap* at Drury Lane Theatre one year a writer observed: "As usual with Mr. Blanchard (the author), the introduction is prefaced by a moral allegory, his object in this case being to show that perfect happiness is by no means the consequence of an ample fortune."

Another pantomime of the instructive type was seen at the Surrey Theatre in 1842. It was called *Lindley Murray's Grammar; or, Harlequin A.E.I.O.U. and Y.*, concerning which one admiring grown-up said: "The subject not only belies the dryness of the cognomen, but it tends very powerfully to show in an amusing form those principles of prudence and morality which are aimed at in the legitimate drama."

The pantomime began in the Halls of Gloom, where a number of sprites and vices were discovered in company with King Ignorance, who, lamenting the march of Intellect, informed his subjects that the Fairy Queen Orthography had been bold enough to fix upon Lindley Murray as the hero of the pantomime. Subsequently the Vowels proved the victors in their encounter with the forces of Ignorance, and the moral having been satisfactorily conveyed, the fun of the Harlequinade began – much to the relief of the youngsters, I expect.

Another good moral lesson was taught in *See-Saw Margery Daw; or, Harlequin Holiday and Ups and Downs* at Drury Lane in 1857, which set out to show "the diversity of character in this life and to prove that whatsoever may be the situation of man, the ups and downs of life are such as to render it necessary that we should be frugal in our habits and also industrious if we are to have health, wealth, and comfort".

But I think if any prize had been awarded for any pantomime calculated to scare the children it should have been given to *Hey Diddle Diddle; or, Harlequin King Nonsense and the Seven Ages of Man* at Drury Lane Theatre in 1855, for it was described as "A Novel and Original, Inductive, Instructive, Anti-hypochondriacal, Periodical, Episodical, Magical, Tragical, Logical, Chronological, Graphical, Choreographical, Philosophical, Cryptographical, Parabolical, Symbolical, Rhythmical, Mimical, Academical, Mechanical, Technical, Pyrotechnical, Historical, Harmonical, Heroical, Typical, Allegorical, Metaphorical, Chimerical,

Satirical, Metrical, Symmetrical, Lyrical, Musical, Practical, Poetical, Whimsical and side-Shakesperean new grand comic Christmas pantomime"!

That was enough to alarm any average child, but perhaps it was not quite so formidable as the description indicated.

When the curtain rose King Nonsense was seen to be surrounded by the heroes and heroines of nursery literature including Little Jack Horner, Red Riding Hood, Simple Simon, Old Mother Hubbard and Little Boy Blue.

King Nonsense spoke thus:

> Behold King Nonsense! Here I fix my throne,
> And rule a realm peculiarly mine own.
> My faithful Sprat – so apt that caught a hearing;
> My Humpty Dumpty, still to walls adhering;
> My Simple Simon, whom the pieman met;
> Tom Tucker, singing for his supper yet;
> Bo Peep, the Little, and Boy Blue who, too,
> Like small Jack Horner, your own trumpets blew;
> With Mother Hubbard and her tormentor,
> Here you see your great original inventor.

The Spirit of Nonsense appeared and bargained for a little more intellect in children's literature, after which figures representing Routine and Redtape came on and were immediately greeted by the execrations of the multitude. Then followed a lot of schoolboy antics, so it is evident that the pantomime was not quite so serious as might have been feared.

Many of the pantomimes of those far-off days bore strange and tongue-twisting titles and of tremendous length. Let me mention a few of them:

Little Dicky Dilver with his Stick of Silver; or, Harlequin Pretty Prince Pretty Boy and the Three Comical Kings.

This is the House That Jack Built; or, Harlequin Pussycat Where Have You Been, the Little Wee Dog and the Good Child's History of England.

Zig Zag the Crooked; or, Harlequin the King, the Cat and the Pretty Princess or the Frog, the Fairy and the Wishes Three.

Harlequin Sun and Moon; or, the Seven Sisters of the Zodiac in an Uproar.

Harlequin and the Five Senses; or, Happy Land and Evil Land and the Union of the Allied Powers in the Realms of Truth and Light.

King Flame and Queen Pearly Drop; or, Harlequin Simple Simon and the Pretty Little Mermaid at the Bottom of the Sea.

The Flying Dutchman; or, Harlequin the Riddle of the Sphinx and the Pretty Princess who was Made by a Charm.

Harlequin and the World of Flowers; or, the Fairy of the Rose and the Sprite of the Silver Star.

Many of the pantomimes were based upon historical subjects, such, for example, as *King Alfred the Great; or, Harlequin History and the Enchanted Raven* at the Olympic Theatre in 1847. It must have been rather confusing to those who were well up in their history, for in one scene Clown appeared as Richard the Third.

In *Alfred the Great and the Magic Banjo and the Magic Raven* at the Marylebone Theatre in 1850 the good king was represented in the famous cake-burning incident, after which he was proclaimed First Lord of the Admiralty and England's forest oaks were changed into the English fleet.

And then, as this was a period very much interested in the progress of science and invention, there were such strange pantomimes as *Harlequin and the Steam Engine; or, Pervonte's Wishes and the Fairy Fog* which showed the construction of trains and workshops in full swing under the guidance of the Railway King; *The Birth of the Steam Engine; or, Harlequin Locomotive and his Men* in which James Watt was the hero who won the blacksmith's pretty daughter as the reward for his invention; *The Land of Light; or, Harlequin Gas and the Four Elements – Earth, Air, Fire and Water*, and also *Harlequin N.E.W.S. and the Fairy Elves of the Fourth Estate*, which had newspapers as its odd theme.

By all this it can be gathered how much the nature of pantomime has changed during a century of its popularity.

9
The Poetry of Pantomime

DURING the period about which I have been writing several notable changes had taken place in pantomime. For one thing it had become the custom for the hero or "principal boy" to be played by a shapely actress instead of by an actor, as had been the early practice. We accept the idea now as quite normal, and it seems quite natural for Prince Charming or Dick Whittington and Aladdin to be impersonated by someone who is obviously a woman, just as we are accustomed to the part of the comical old woman or "dame" being played by a man. This exchange of roles is only one of the many odd things about such a typically British institution as the pantomime we know.

It is generally agreed that the first actual principal boy was Miss Ellington, who appeared as the Prince in *The Good Woman in the Wood* at the Lyceum Theatre in 1852.

For a long period the pantomime formed only one part of the programme, for it was customary until close on 1880 to precede it with a comedy or serious play, even Shakespeare, the pantomime forming a kind of dessert in the evening's entertainment.

But as the tendency grew to develop the fairy-tale portion of the pantomime, rather than to rely upon Clown and the Harlequinade, the pantomimes improved in quality. Among those who contributed more than anyone of his time to this improvement was E. L. Blanchard, who was probably responsible for more productions than any other author. The record of this genial writer who gave so much to children's entertainment was really quite remarkable. From 1852 until 1888 he was the author of every Drury Lane pantomime, or "Annuals" as in his old fashioned way he preferred to call them. They were full of fun and frolic, marked with pleasant wit and graceful poetry and all were without a touch of vulgarity such as, I fear, marred some of the pantomimes of his time.

Such was his ingenuity that he contrived to make pretty and interesting stories out of such unlikely and difficult subjects as *Goody Two Shoes, See-Saw Margery Daw, The House that Jack Built* and *Little Jack Horner*.

His smooth verse, his happy dialogue, his charming imagery and playfulness, made such delightful reading that one could forgive him for his tendency to include moral lessons in what he wrote. "As an exponent of fairy mythology for the little ones," wrote one admirer, "he was the Countess d'Aulnois, Perrault, and the Brothers Grimm rolled into one."

Born in 1820 Blanchard, who was the son of an actor, wrote his first pantomime, when a youth of only seventeen, for a private performance. It was called *The Old Woman and Her Three Sons; or, Harlequin and the Wizard of Wookey Hole*. He not only wrote the pantomime, but he played the Harlequin and on one occasion he even deputised as Columbine.

Brought up in the atmosphere of the stage, he knew all about pantomime from A to Z. Between the ages of seventeen and twenty he wrote as many as thirty plays. His first professional pantomime was *Jack and the Beanstalk*, which was produced at the Royal Victoria Theatre (later known as the Old Vic) in 1844, and he modestly hid his identity under the name of Francesco Frost. Later on he sometimes wrote under the name of the Brothers Grinn. In 1847 he supplied the pantomimes at three theatres.

One year he was the author of no fewer than five pantomimes at different theatres. He displayed such industry and gave so much pleasure to the public that he deserved to be better rewarded. Sometimes he received only £20 or so for his Drury Lane pantomime, and it is therefore not surprising that he died quite a poor man.

His first pantomime at Drury Lane was in 1852 and it was entitled *Harlequin Hudibras; or, Old Dame Durden and the*

Droll Days of the Merry Monarch. It was described as being "full of those amiable inconsistencies which endear farce to the heart of childhood. Mr. Blanchard has mixed up Charles the Second, Hudibras and Dame Durden for no imaginable purpose but to make fun of them and in this he succeeds."

The pantomime introduced ghosts, goblins, Antiquity and the Spirit of Improvement and the Crystal Palace (which was then the latest novelty in London), thronged with a troupe of dancers. King Charles went through the adventures of the Penderel Oak and was finally crowned in Cheapside. King Charles became Harlequin subsequently and Hudibras was turned into Clown.

King Charles made his entry disguised as Sir Rowley, crying:

> Oddsfish, Sir Lambkin, these are pleasant quarters
> Thanks to the sun that lit us to these daughters.
> I will stop here and in the farmyard loiter,
> Whilst you go round about and reconnoitre.

After which King Charles, seeing a loaf, cheese and ale prepared for breakfast, is proceeding to demolish it when Alice comes from the door of the house. She is crossing the stage as Charles, struck by her beauty, accosts her:

CHARLES. Turn, lovely fair! That form has something in it
　Which made me love you from the first-last minute.
ALICE.　　And pray, sir, who are you?
CHARLES.　　　　　　　　　　 – Fair maid, you see
　One who is, ahem! who, is I may say, me.
　My name is Rowley, whilst this I *am* on
　Believe your Rowley-Powley free from gammon.

Then Dame Durden enters:

DAME.　　A lover in my absence?　Girl, explain,
　　And cavaliers don't cavilling here remain,
　　But quick, be off!
CHARLES.　　　　　　　　　 – Oddsfish, we've caught a tartar;
DAME.　　You soldiers dart in everybody's *darter.*

As an example of Blanchard's industry I may mention that in 1852, in addition to supplying Drury Lane with its pantomime he also wrote *Harlequin and the World of Flowers* for the Surrey Theatre, *Undine and the Spirit of Water* for the Marylebone Theatre, as well as lending a hand in the Princess's Theatre pantomime, writing a song for Flexmore the Clown and inventing the comic business for the Harlequinade in a Liverpool pantomime.

I could go on for a long time picking out little gems of verse and humour from Blanchard's pantomime books. To give you an idea of his neat invention let us turn to *Jack and the Beanstalk; or, Harlequin and the Merry Pranks of the Good Little People*, which was played at Drury Lane in 1859.

The first scene took place in "The Atmosphere 45 miles above the Earth's surface" where Weather arrived, attended by Heat and Cold, in her Aurora Borealis car, and this is some of the dialogue:

> WEATHER. No, I'm the one that puzzles you, the Weather!
> In vain you have tried to guess me – don't be vexed,
> Nobody knows what I may turn out next.
> I hardly know myself – you well may stare.
> ZADKIEL.   All that I know is, you are very fair.
> WEATHER. That's very fair of you, but not surprising,
> When my barometer you saw was rising.
> But where in England can you rest or walk about
> Without my being the subject people talk about?
> To me each morn they pay their first attention
> When folks converse the Weather they first mention.
> In every zone, from arctic to the tropic,
> I'm every day the universal topic.

"But why this feminine appearance?" asks the puzzled Zadkiel, to which Weather replies:

> I'm like a woman, changeable you know.
> Around me here my aerial agents view:
> Snow, Hail and Sleet and Mist and Rain and Dew.
> They do a good deal in their small way,
> Though sometimes inconvenient, I must say.

From the Illustrated Sporting and Dramatic News

FAIRYLAND SCENE IN "CINDERELLA" AT DRURY LANE THEATRE, 1879

Constant attendants on me, you behold
My faithful ministers in heat and cold.
Each looks upon his fellow as a brother:
In fact, one can't exist without the other.

After much more of that sort of thing the familiar story of
Jack and the Beanstalk was unfolded.

There was a pretty scene in the Grotto of the Pixies, in
which Prism, Queen of the Fairies, addressing her subjects,
said:

Poor mortals, some amongst them have insisted
No giants in this country e'er existed.
Their incredulity so far may go.
To doubt if fairies ever lived or no.
We live and let live – that's the elfin motto;
"With song and dance now cheer our moonlit grotto."

Then Queen Prism sings this charming little song:

Oh, this is our haunt when the stars shine bright,
    And blithe are the strains of the fairies' song;
Whilst echoes that lurk in the shadows of night
    Respond to the lay of the elfin throng.
Hither we troop, when the moon is veiled.
    And shineth the meteor's light alone;
Weaving a spell for the swain that failed
    To keep his troth to the plighted one.
        For never did tryst or trust go wrong,
        Without the wrath of the elfin throng.

Merrily thus do we fairies live!
    To be free as the air is our elfin boast;
And, true to our mission, we secretly give
    A help to the one that may need it the most.
Then hither we troop, when the moon shines bright.
    To tell what deeds are worthily done;
And we weave a spell from her silver light,
    That shall aid the cause of the virtuous one.
        For never did truth to youth belong
        Without reward from the elfin throng.

E

When Jack goes to market to sell the cow he meets a
young farmer who is the fairy Crystalline in disguise. When
he is offered the magic beans in exchange he exclaims:

> What pretty beans! Ah, I must mind, likewise
> My P's and Q's, as well as beans and eyes.
> What strange odd fancies come upon me gazing;
> A fascination they possess amazing;
> They have a kind of magic look about them;
> It seems as if I couldn't be without them,
> And anything would give to call them mine.

CRYSTALLINE. Well, give the calf.
JACK.   I do!
CRYSTALLINE. The beans are thine.
JACK.   Though this transaction bears a strange character
               I look upon you as my beany-factor.

When later on Jack breaks the news to his mother she
cries:

> Incredible! Impossible! What, dispose of
> A splendid calf to no one that one knows of!
> A calf, one of the regular twenty stunners,
> For half a dozen seeds of scarlet runners;
> I feel my back comb rising perpendicular,
> And each grey hair to stand on end particular.

The magic beanstalk is made to grow by Fairy Prism and
her attendant pixies, who respond to her call:

> Come, tricksy pixies, from each bush and briar,
> Ere morning light compels you to retire,
> Ye hovering round, by mortal eye unseen,
> Who have ever watchful o'er their actions been,
> Who mark each turn of fortune and direct it,
> Still at their elbow when they least expect it.
> Whilst April showers assist your work below.
> Appear and make the magic beanstalk grow.

There was a very charming scene with the fairies in *The
White Cat* at Drury Lane in 1878 after the Wicked Fairy had
worked her evil spells. Fairy Mysotis entered crying:

Flower fairies from the brake,
Water lilies from the lake!
Hasten to this sylvan spot,
Help I need. Forget-me-not!

When the fairies entered this was their pretty dialogue:

MYSOTIS.   Thanks for your aid! A welcome each receives,
While this soft moonlight falls upon your leaves,
A tale I must unfold.
VERONICA.   Don't say a word,
There's not a flower but knows what has occurred.
CELANDINE. White roses who were present at the feast
Have told us everything they knew at least.
MYSOTIS.   What, of the birthday?
VERONICA.   Oh, much more than that:
How the Princess was changed into a cat.
CELANDINE. And how the wicked fairy came and then
Carried her off from all the nice young men.
VERONICA.   Because she wouldn't wed the fairy's son,
Psycho, the ugly!
MYSOTIS.   Then my story's done!
CELANDINE. Where leaves can whisper and where breeze has
blown,
Through Europe by this time the tale is known.
VERONICA.   In bramble thicket and on hedgerows hawked
about,
There's nothing but this White Cat's story talked about.
MYSOTIS.   As what has happened all here seem to know
My little speech will not much longer grow.
To rescue the Princess we all must haste,
She never plucked a flower in wanton waste.
Cherishing those she liked, she snipped them shorter
But gave them plenty of fresh air and water.
CELANDINE.   Here every flower will render you assistance.
VERONICA.   We'll make the monster keep his proper distance.
MYSOTIS.   Our spirit power is limited understand,
We only can materialise a Hand!
But soon the White Cat's castle comes in sight
If with these hands we guide the Princess right.
If in that form one loves her – there's no harm,
Offer of marriage will break the witch's charm.
CELANDINE. Our hands are at your service!
VERONICA.   All agreed!

MYSOTIS.   Then let the Princes on their path proceed,
While we, as fairy books all say we do,
Punish the wicked and protect the true!
CELANDINE. If we accomplish this performance well
The task you set us will be bagatelle.

One of the curious things about these old pantomimes is
that a great deal of time was spent in the introductory
scenes, in which demon kings and fairy queens or some such
spirits would argue about the subject to be chosen for the
pantomime. It often seemed as if half the pantomime was
over before the subject of the evening's entertainment had
been decided upon.

Here, for instance, is an extract from an opening scene in
*Little Jack Horner and the Princess Esmeralda; or, Harlequin
Number Nip and the Magic Plum*, which was performed in
Manchester in 1873.

A great deal of argument goes on between Father Time,
Discordia, a wicked fairy and Harmonia (who, naturally, is
peacefully inclined), as to what the subject of the pantomime
shall be. At length Discordia says impatiently:

> Now then, to work, we have no time to lose,
> And first a victim I must choose,
> One of Harmonia's set (so I may scorn her)
> None could be better than her pet Jack Horner.
> Krosspatch attend, haste to his mother's dwelling
> There with your spells so spoil the lot, in brief
> For making Christmas pies she's all excelling;
> That Holloway or Cockle* shall yield no relief.
> That being done, there is no question
> Discordia's best friend is Indigestion.

Thereupon Harmonia enters, saying:

> What's this I hear, plotting against dear Jack?
> Well, never mind, I'll soon be on your track,
> And with my counter spells disarm your scheming
> I've powerful aid, of which you're little dreaming.
> What ho! good Number Nip straightway appear.
>   (*enter* Number Nip).
> You're wanted quickly – there is danger near.

* Patent medicines.—AUTHOR.

Good Jack Horner, that very best of boys,
Who all my constant care and love enjoys;
Haste to his home and in his Christmas pie
Place this charmed plum – don't ask the *raisin* why.

Then again there is the dramatic opening to *Jack and Jill
and the Well on the Hill; or, The House that Jack Built*, which
was played at the Surrey Theatre in 1883.

The scene is "a weird and weedy wood" and when the
evil spirits Falsehood, Fable and Fiction enter the following
dialogue is heard:

FALSEHOOD. Fable and Fiction! Falsehood gives ye greeting,
Dame Nature favours this our nightly meeting;
'Tis dark and drear, befitting darkest deeds,
FABLE. That we implant and reap among the weeds –
(*pointing to well*)
And we've done *well* for we've dried it up,
It's water now would fail to fill a cup.
(*Enter* FACT, FUN and FANCY.)
FACT. Say you so? Not so fast my kings,
You know the proverb: "Facts are stubborn things;"
And I'm a stubborn fact, so cease you action.
FALSEHOOD. To *shun* such facts would give me satis*factshun*.
What want you here?
FACT. I'll answer for the youth,
He comes to clear the weed-grown well of Truth.
FALSEHOOD. You'd better *let well alone!*
FACT. We to break the spell come –
Come Fairy of the *Well*, we give you *welcome!*
TRUTH. I breathe again, and thank my constant friends,
My long imprisonment by their aid ends;
Though Falsehood may prevail for a period brief,
Yet Time to Truth will sometimes give relief,
For Truth will out.
FALSEHOOD. Ha! Ha! our flag's unfurled,
And waves in triumph over half the lying world.
With rich or poor we play our little lark;
Even on *princes* Falsehood *prints his* mark.
We have set our mark on one right royal youth,
Who, strange to say, can seldom speak the truth.
TRUTH. Our's be the task to break this hateful spell
With water pure from Truth's enchanted well.
Tell me the Prince's name!

FACT.   As he's such a shammer,
  He's known in general as "the young Prince Crammer."
TRUTH. I have a favourite youth – a sailor, too
  Who speaks the truth and shames the likes of you.
  Aye, laugh your loudest now, the time will come
  When baffled rage will leave you silent – dumb.
FALSEHOOD. I defy your power!
FACT.   Defy away, old friend.
TRUTH.   Then it's war between us?
FALSEHOOD. To the bitter end.

Many of these discussions reveal a great deal about the topics and fashions of the times. For example, take the following scene from Blanchard's *King Humming-Top* at Drury Lane Theatre in 1853 and you will note, among other things, a reference to beards, a fashion that was encouraged by the unshaven soldiers returning from the war in the Crimea:

FASHION.   In my department, I ought to say,
  Short sleeves for mantles now have had their day.
  For the material velvet is preferred,
  Trimmed *à la Turque* with –
NOVELTY.   Not another word.
  At lady's bonnets men appear to scoff.
FASHION.   I admit there is a little *falling-off*.
  But to the other sex I've caused a little saving
  By getting men to leave off shaving.
SUCCESS.   Which I've made so successful that you trace
  A photograph of Beard's in every face.
INVENTION. Whilst I've invented plans with assiduity
  And engines of the greatest ingenuity;
  But since in fun there's been so great a call,
  To invent a joke's the hardest thing of all.
FASHION.   That's news indeed: From all it would appear
  You've really had enough to do this year.
NOVELTY.   Well, what with submarine electric cables,
  Mysterious rappings from revolving tables,
  Sewing machines that steam at work will keep
  And so enable those who sew to reap.
  With other marvels of a late invention
  That now are much too numerous to mention,

I really think – to quote a famous poet –
I've done the State some service and they know it.
No more of that. But yet – so strange to see –
One novelty astounded even me.
FASHION.   And that was –
NOVELTY.   Drury Lane crammed every night
By one Shakesperean actor. That is quite
A novel feature – really does you credit –
Nay, Fashion, you deserve my praise – I've said it;
Whilst actors who can really act arise,
The good old English drama never dies.

Though Blanchard was one of the most industrious writers of pantomime there were many rivals in the field. One of the most active of them was Nelson Lee, who was described by Thackeray as "the author of I don't know how many hundred glorious pantomimes – walking by the summer wave at Margate or Brighton, perhaps revolving in his mind the idea of some gorgeous new spectacle of faëry which this winter shall complete". In one year (1850) he provided the pantomimes for nine London and provincial theatres, including Drury Lane, the Marylebone and the City of London, where he was in management for fifteen years.

Lee, who was the son of a naval officer, took to the stage very early in life and at times appeared as Clown, Harlequin and Pantaloon, so he had a thorough practical knowledge of what pantomime should be.

Another busy writer was Frank W. Green, who wrote many pantomimes for the Surrey Theatre and was noted for his habit of punning in the days when that literary habit was peculiarly rife. Here is an example from *Jack and Jill; or, Harlequin Sing-a-Song-of-Sixpence:*

MAID. Three sheets blew off the line; the queen unkind
Declared I was three sheets in the wind.
This wretched maid racked her poor brains
To count her sheets but cannot *count 'er pains.*
JILL. Pray do not weep, although the fates are tricky.
MAID. Yes, everything is looking very dicky.

JILL. To fret o'er little troubles is all bosh.
MAID. Oh that be darned, that sort of thing wont wash.
JILL. We're going to take a shop when Jack's been paid.
MAID. But where are you going to get the *stockin'* trade?

Here, as another specimen of Green's rhymes, is an extract from the speech of one of his demon kings:

Yes, I'm the Demon Butcher; it is I
Who keeps the price of meat precious high;
'Tis I who cause the cattle to be ill,
And with bad meat the market-places fill;
The rise of milk to fivepence was my doing;
I love to see folks come to rack and ruin.
In short, at every mischief I'm a sad 'un,
And you may write me down a right down bad 'un.

Puns, indeed, were considered an essential part of every pantomime. Listen to what a princess had to say in a Manchester pantomime:

Cease, oh cease! for at your endless *railing*
My spirits sink, my very cheeks are *paling*.
Why will you still those doleful *changes* ring
That *chime* hot with my thoughts, you tiresome thing?
Then of my faults you've told me oft, you scold;
A young *belle* like me need not be always *told*.

But the greatest of all punsters of a period when puns were so much in fashion was Henry J. Byron, the journalist and writer of many popular burlesques and farces, who introduced the habit of playing such tricks with the Queen's English into everything he published. In one of his pantomimes about *Dick Whittington*, Alderman Fitzwarren had this to say:

Fitzwarren's togs are all *fits-warranted*
And an inspection humbly we request.
There's nowhere in Eastcheap such prime *cheap wests*.

In the same pantomime the Princess at one point exclaimed:

Put up your scimitar; if at once it flies out
You must prepare to *see me tear* your eyes out.

I fear that a good deal of this sort of humour must have been quite incomprehensible not only to the children but to the most sophisticated and quick-witted grown-ups in the audience.

Pantomime Subjects

ROUND about the 'seventies of the last century one notable change began to affect the character of pantomime. Hitherto the authors had covered a wide field for their subjects and had invented all sorts of strange and fantastic stories for them. But now, with all the fineries made available by scene-designing, stage mechanism and improved lighting, they began to restrict themselves in the way of subjects to those few favourite stories such as *Cinderella, Dick Whittington, The Babes in the Wood, Mother Goose, Aladdin* and *Jack and the Beanstalk* which are still popular in these days. The specially invented stories began to be discarded by all but one or two theatres, notably the Britannia Theatre, Hoxton, and the Grecian Theatre, which stood in City Road.

The most notable of the purely English contributions to the list of pantomime subjects are *Dick Whittington and His Cat, The Babes in the Wood, Robinson Crusoe, St. George and the Dragon* and *Gulliver's Travels* (both long ago abandoned as subjects) and *Little Goody Two Shoes*.

Many of the fairy-tales popular in this country came into England after being first presented at the French Court. These pretty folk tales were put into graceful literary form by Charles Perrault. His tales in *Contes de ma Mère l'Oie* (Tales of Mother Goose) included *The Sleeping Beauty, Red Riding Hood and the Wolf, Bluebeard, Puss in Boots, Diamonds and Toads, Cinderella, Ricquet with the Tuft* and *Hop o' My Thumb*. These stories were soon translated into English, and most of them have formed the subjects of pantomime.

The story of *Red Riding Hood*, which some learned writers have traced back to the days of the Roman Emperor Nero, found its way into Germany and was utilised by the Brothers Grimm.

Puss in Boots was derived by Perrault from a book entitled *Nights of Straporola* which appeared in Italy in 1534. It is also found in the German collection of stories by Ludwig Tieck. In most versions the cat is a clever creature who, by his wit and cunning, induces his master to pass himself off as the Marquis de Carabas with very profitable and romantic results. The story is known among Indian and African tribes.

In the Hungarian version of the story there is a fox instead of a cat. A poor miller saves him from the hunters and the fox gives him copper and gold and offers to get him a wife.

Sleeping Beauty was derived by Perrault from a Persian story.

Bluebeard has been identified as the notorious Gilles de Retz, Marquis de Laval, Marshal of France, who, it is recorded, murdered six out of seven of his wives and was eventually executed in 1440. In the pantomime, however, the tale has nearly always been given an Oriental setting, probably because similar incidents in the story occur in the tale of the Third Kalendar in the *Arabian Nights*. The story is really not a suitable subject for such a jolly thing as pantomime and many managers regard it as very unlucky and refuse to stage it.

Perrault's charming story of *Riquet with the Tuft* was once a great favourite for pantomime, but it is many years since it has been seen in England.

About the same time that Perrault became known in England the tales of the French Countess d'Aulnois were introduced here. Her stories include *The Yellow Dwarf*, *Goldilocks* and *The White Cat*, all of which became popular as pantomime subjects, though nowadays they are seldom used.

The Babes in the Wood first made its appearance in England about five hundred years ago. The story is founded on fact and was first put into ballad form in *The Children of the Wood; or, the Norfolk Gentleman's Last Will and Testament.* The tragedy of the babes is said to have happened in Norfolk and the scene where they are covered with leaves by the robins has been identified as Waylands Wood. According to local tradition the ghosts of the poor children can still be heard crying there.

In pantomime the babes are generally associated with Robin Hood, who rescues them. According to popular legend, Robin Hood lived two or three hundred years before the babes had their adventure, but, of course, one mustn't expect little things like that to worry the writers of pantomime. As far as I can discover Robin Hood first intruded into the story of the babes in the Covent Garden pantomime of 1857.

By the way, it was then noted, I am sorry to say, that the babes were "noisy, mischievous, destructive and in all respects tormenting; they smash china, glass, furniture and all kinds of property that when demolished comes under the general heading of 'breakery'; skip in the drawing-room, squirt water in everybody's face, perplex the cook and in a hundred other ways, exasperate their uncle."

The Arabian Nights, of which the first English translation appeared in 1704-17, contributed the popular subjects of *Aladdin, Sinbad the Sailor*, and *Ali Baba and the Forty Thieves*, which is also regarded as an unlucky subject by the producers.

Aladdin was the first of the stories to be seen on the stage, though it was the subject not of a pantomime, but of a serious play. That was at Covent Garden Theatre in 1788. When it was produced there again in 1813 Grimaldi appeared as the dumb slave Kasrac, a character which has since disappeared from the pantomime version.

We owe *Cinderella*, the most popular and charming of all pantomime subjects, to France, though there are said to be at least four hundred different versions of the story. It has been described as the greatest story in the world, and certainly it is one of the oldest, for it can be traced back many centuries and it is probably prehistoric.

Children all over the world are familiar with the story. The Rumanians know the little cinder-maiden as "the Emperor's daughter in a pigsty"; the Russians have naturalised her as "Mar with smuts on her nose". In the Swedish version an ox helps her, supplies her with rich dresses and carries her to court on its back.

It is curious that in nearly every version of the story in its early form the ugly sisters cut off their toes and heels in order to fit the slipper, but that device is never suggested in pantomime.

What was Cinderella's slipper really made of? Many learned folk say it should be one of fur, but in spite of this Perrault wrote *verre* (glass), and glass is surely much more charming for the purpose of pantomime.

Cinderella was first seen on the stage at Drury Lane in 1804, but not in pantomime form. The theatre had to wait until 1864 for the real pantomime treatment of the most popular of all pantomime subjects.

Various changes have been made in the story since that time. That sprightly young fellow Dandini, the valet who always exchanges roles with the Prince, has not always figured in the story. The character was borrowed from Rossini's opera *Cenerentola*.

Very close in order of popularity to *Cinderella* comes *Dick Whittington and His Cat*. *Cinderella* may be the girls' undisputed favourite but I think if an inquiry were made among boys *Dick Whittington* would probably head the list. It may be called London's own pantomime and it is a pleasant mixture of fact and fiction. It was first performed as a pantomime at Covent Garden in 1814.

Richard Whittington was a real personage in City life and was thrice Lord Mayor of London, the last time in 1419. Moreover, he did marry his employer's daughter, Alice Fitzwarren. He died in 1423.

It is not true, however, that he was a poor boy. He was

the son of a well-to-do country gentleman and he was apprenticed to a silk merchant in the City. He did not hear the bells say "Turn again Dick Whittington, thrice Lord Mayor of London" on Highgate Hill, though a stone marks the spot where, according to legend, he rested.

No one knows who invented the picturesque cat part of the story. Various ingenious explanations are given. On a very old building in the City there is (or was) a stone carving of Whittington with his cat. It may be a sign that he used or a crest. Another explanation is that it may have been the name of a ship with which Whittington used to trade with Morocco and which brought him his fortune. A further possible reason is that the word "cat" is confused with the old English word "acate", meaning apparently, a good bargain, or with the French word "achat", which means "purchase" or "buying". Still another theory is that coal ships were known as "cats" in Whittington's day.

Other countries have had their own Whittington stories and it is possible that we have borrowed the cat element from them. One version of the story was published sixty years before Whittington was born. There is a Portuguese version concerning the son of a poor woman who embarked for India with his cat. At the time of his arrival the King's palace was overrun with rats and mice. The widow's son let loose his cat among them, clearing the place of vermin, and the King bought the cat for a large sum, enabling its lucky owner to return home with a fortune.

As early as 1604 a play on the subject was licensed in England and there are allusions to the story from 1660 onwards.

The story follows familiar lines in these days, but it differs somewhat from the earlier pantomimic versions. In a Drury Lane production of 1835 the pantomime opened in the orthodox way in Fitzwarren's kitchen, and Dick, in his master's absence, was subjected to the persecutions of Dame Suett, the cook. The tale took an unfamiliar turn on the arrival of Fitzwarren, who had made a fortune for Dick with the aid of his cat. In spite of Dick's newly acquired wealth Fitzwarren wished to marry his daughter to the son of Alderman Gobble. At this awkward juncture the Genius of Industry intervened on Dick's behalf and made a general change of the characters into those of the Harlequinade.

In a pantomime at Astley's in 1877 the story of Dick Whittington was combined with that of John Gilpin and his ride to Edmonton.

The story of *Beauty and the Beast* is known in many countries. As told among the Basques it concerns a king who, on leaving his home, asks his three daughters what he shall bring them on his return. The youngest asks for a flower. When the king is plucking the flower he hears a voice asking him what he is doing and telling him that he must bring one of his daughters to the castle.

The youngest daughter goes to the castle and sleeps there. Next morning she hears a voice crying: "I wish to place my head upon her knees." The voice is that of an enormous serpent who subsequently turns into a beautiful young man. He had been transformed into a serpent until some woman would love him in that repellent form.

The Hungarian version introduces a pig who helps the king out of his difficulties on condition that he is given the youngest daughter. A somewhat similar story is found in Polish, Tyrolese, Italian and Lithuanian versions.

The pantomime subject of *Robinson Crusoe* is, of course, founded on Defoe's story, which in turn was founded upon the adventures of Alexander Selkirk, a young sailor who was marooned on the lonely island of Juan Fernandez. In its original form *Robinson Crusoe* has no fairy or romantic element, but the story has been standardised into one in which the hero's mother and his sweetheart Polly Perkins as well as the pirate Will Atkins, are introduced. It was first performed as pantomime at Drury Lane Theatre in 1781.

In a version produced at the Standard Theatre in the 'seventies Crusoe was played by a man, and in the end he was unromantically married to a widow.

In a version played at Drury Lane Theatre, Blanchard introduced hitherto unrecorded incidents into the story. Mrs. Crusoe came up to London with her son and established the Primrose Farm dairy on the banks of the Thames, to the intense disgust of her neighbour, with whose daughter her son was in love.

While *Robinson Crusoe* is popular enough among the grown-ups, it is least popular among the children, for an obvious reason: It is impossible to stick to Defoe's story. There are no women in the original tale, but it is impossible to make a pantomime without them. So the tale has to be altered, and children look somewhat askance at the introduction of Mrs. Crusoe, Will Atkins, the villain of the piece, and Polly Perkins who is Crusoe's sweetheart, a fact which Defoe managed to omit from his story. All the children want is the story of Robinson Crusoe on his island and Man Friday. Any variation is likely to puzzle them.

Jack the Giant Killer is a version of the old English legend of Coroneus the Trojan, companion of the Trojan Brutus when he first landed in Britain. But Jack will continue to be regarded as one of the valiant Cornishmen who did so much towards ridding Wales of its giants.

Jack and the Beanstalk has likewise to do with a giant, but it is a much prettier story and much more adapted to the purposes of a pantomime. The English story is practically unique in the introduction of the magic beans, but the theme of a bad bargain over the sale of a cow is known in many other versions. Sometimes the hero is ruined as a result of the deal; sometimes, as in the English version, it turns his fortune.

Puss in Boots was first performed as a pantomime in 1817 and *Red Riding Hood* (as *Rodolph the Wolf; or, Columbine Red Riding Hood*) in the following year.

Little Goody Two Shoes, which is sometimes used as a pantomime subject, is founded on the story written in 1765 by Oliver Goldsmith. So slight are some of the other subjects which have been used by pantomime writers and so thin the fable in which they are concerned that they have often been spoiled by being combined in one confusing mixture. It must have puzzled many children in the past to find that Little Bo-Peep was Jack Horner's sweetheart or that Goody Two Shoes was the playmate of Little Boy Blue. It would be no more surprising to learn that Cinderella intended to marry Aladdin or that Mrs. Crusoe was the object of Bluebeard's devotion.

11

Clown Fades Away

I HAVE described certain changes and developments in pantomime and now I must add something about a further change that considerably altered the old-fashioned kind of pantomime which, as it was known in mid-Victorian times, was quite a simple kind of entertainment, intended to appeal to the children rather than to the grown-ups. As I have already noted, it was customary at one time to precede the pantomime with a serious play, the latter part of the evening's entertainment being added during the Christmas holiday season.

As you will have seen, the old-fashioned pantomimes were very simple in their appeal – just a little fairy-story or nursery-tale unfolded with dialogue in verse, some pretty songs and music and a good deal of magic, all of which was followed by the more boisterous fun of the Harlequinade, which many of the grown-ups tolerated only for the sake of the children, who certainly enjoyed it.

Somewhere between 1860 and 1870 the managements decided that the pantomime itself – not the Harlequinade – needed some sort of brightening-up, with more knockabout fun than had been the custom. So it came about that many of them began to introduce music-hall artists into the performance.

One of the first of the music-hall comedians to be engaged was G. H. Macdermott, who, with his rousing songs, was very popular among London audiences. He was engaged to play Bluff King Hal in *Herne the Hunter* at the Grecian Theatre in 1870, and later on he appeared in *The Black Statue* at the Britannia Theatre, on which occasion somebody wrote: "He can dance and sing. His first accomplishment is rewarded with thunders of applause, while his vocal gifts, being employed upon melodies which all who hear can echo, there was frequently the accompaniment of a thousand voices by way of chorus."

Another pioneer of the invasion from the music hall was an excellent comedian named James Fawn, who died in 1923 and is therefore still remembered by many present-day playgoers. It was he who, in *The Children of the Wood* at the Adelphi Theatre in 1874, introduced the once very popular song "Tommy Make Room for Your Uncle".

For seven or eight years he was a great success at Drury Lane Theatre with that racy and highly popular comedian Arthur Roberts, and their topical songs were always an enjoyable part of the show. One of Fawn's best-known songs was "If You Want to Know the Time Ask a Policemen", which held its popularity for many years.

In 1874 Harry Nicholls, a big, jolly-faced comedian, appeared at the Surrey Theatre as a "dame". Then he went to the Grecian Theatre, where he met Herbert Campbell, who was also a stoutly built comedian, and later on they both appeared at Drury Lane Theatre together.

And so from that time onwards the music-hall artists, women as well as men, monopolised the best parts in the pantomime, making it something which the grown-ups could enjoy just as much as the children. Indeed, I fancy that a good deal of what was introduced did not appeal so much to younger minds as did all the pretty fairy business which so often got crowded out. The comedians brought with them from the many variety halls of the day their own robust and rowdy funny business, their own jokes and songs, and introduced much that did not appear in the pantomime dialogue written by the authors. As someone complained, save for what the Fairy Queen uttered you could hardly be sure that anything you heard came from the poor author.

This new kind of pantomime was not welcomed by many people who preferred the simpler, more graceful, poetic and fairylike kind of entertainment that they had enjoyed in their childhood.

One well-known dramatic critic, W. Davenport Adams, was particularly wrathful about the change that had come over the Christmas entertainment, for in 1882 he made a vigorous attack upon what he had seen in the various London theatres.

He complained of the monotony of the subjects treated, of the restricted range of stories, and protested against the liberties with which the cherished nursery legends were treated.

"Now to what do we owe this unfortunate, nay painful feature of pantomime performances?" he asked. "I fear there can be but one answer to the question. We owe it to the music-hall element among the performers."

Then he added, after denouncing a lot of things that he had noticed: "Why must the hero always be a woman dressed in tights and tunic? And why must the comic old woman always be a man? Have we not plenty of youthful premiers and female comedians?"

He said that he could not see how pantomime could continue to hold its own unless it mended its way, but in that respect he was not a very good prophet, for, whether he was right or wrong in some of the matters to which he objected, pantomime has continued to be very popular with children as well as their elders in very much the same form as he saw it.

It was not only in respect of music-hall comedians and their humour that pantomime was changing. Mechanical wonders and scene-painting had so developed and improved that the human artists were sometimes in danger of being swamped by too much extravagance and magnificence.

One writer in 1877 seemed quite alarmed by the change.

"Pantomime," he said, "is dying on account of the marvellous complexity of mechanism, painting, limelight, coloured fire and ballet girls which form what we call a transformation scene. Upon this one effect depends success or failure. Dancers, singers, plot and pantomimists are all secondary to this consideration. The glories of the Clown and Harlequinade pale before their brilliance, and pantomime as our fathers and grandfathers knew it is a thing of the past."

Another writer of about the same period almost deplored the popularity of this new kind of pantomime. "In London," he wrote, "Harlequin is an ornament of the season like glittering hoar frost; in East London he is an idol. Pass beyond the suburbs and push onwards to any extremity of the island in which a theatre is to be found and there the Christmas pantomime, well got up according to local resources, is to be found in its proper season. This wide spread of pantomime in the provinces is a comparatively new feature in the history of the English drama, and certain it is that this species of entertainment, although Italian in its origin, has become as natural to the unsophisticated playgoer as the Oriental turkey is to every Briton who tastes his Christmas dinner."

Now, there is one particularly sad feature about all this. The introduction of the funny men from the music halls marked the beginning of the end of the long reign of popularity enjoyed by the Clown and his companions. It meant the doom of the old-fashioned Harlequinade and all its simple fun which had been the custom since the days of Grimaldi.

It is true that the end was still a long way off and that for many years Clown would go through his time-honoured business of stealing legs of mutton and sausages, of tormenting tradesmen and leading the policeman a dance. For a long time the transformation scene would end the fairy-tale part of the pantomime and, with brilliant displays of red and green fire, the Harlequinade company would appear on the stage at the bidding of the Fairy Queen. For many years Clown would enter with his cheery cry of "Here we are again!" and would greet old Pantaloon with "Hullo, father!" after having wished the audience "A muddy

Christmas and a sloppy New Year!" Harlequin would still go on performing surprising changes with a slap of his magic bat and Columbine would go on pirouetting in her pretty, gossamer-like way.

But all this sort of thing began to lose its importance. Clown was no longer the hero of the evening and the admired idol of the children. His place was rapidly being taken by the comedians. They even stole his tricks and his fun. They robbed him of much of the "comic business" that made the children laugh, and he was therefore given less and less to do.

Poor old Clown! What would Grimaldi have thought of the sad decline of the Harlequinade, the jolly business of which he had invented?

So from the time that the music-hall comedians came on to the scene the Harlequinade, which had once occupied the better and the most exciting and important part of the evening and had once been carried through in as many as half a dozen scenes, began to shrink into just one or two changes. For years the Harlequinade was carried on in many pantomimes in one short scene in front of the traditional row of shops. Poor Clown did his best to carry on, and there were still many favourites in the part but, with his red-hot poker and his old-time fun, he was fighting a losing battle against the new style of pantomime which despised his simple foolery.

Clowns like Harry Payne and Whimsical Walker at Drury Lane, like George Lupino at the Britannia Theatre, and many others in London and the provinces, bravely strove to keep the flag of Grimaldi flying. But they were given less and less chance. At Drury Lane the Harlequinade dwindled into a single scene during which (no doubt to the distress of many of the children) the grown-ups, too much concerned with the lateness of the hour and with the necessity of catching trains and of getting their young charges to bed at a reasonable hour, began to collect wraps and coats and were impatient at the delay that poor Joey was causing. Finally all that Clown did was to appear on the stage and distribute some Christmas crackers among a few fortunate children in the audience before the curtain came down.

How sad it is to read that some people rejoiced in this decay of the Harlequinade. One newspaper critic heartlessly wrote: "The Harlequinade is very short and that is by no means a disadvantage. Much of the buffoonery once popular in this species of entertainment in the present day is voted wearisome." And that was written despite the fact that the Clown of the occasion was Harry Payne.

Drury Lane entirely abandoned the Harlequinade long before its final pantomime, but here and there in London and the provinces Clowns lingered on the scene for a few years, encouraged by a few managements who still had respect for ancient tradition. But Clowns were a diminishing band and there were few left who could be relied upon to supply the kind of fun in which at one time so many had specialised.

The last of the London theatres where Clown lingered was the Lyccum, which closed its doors as a theatre when the 1939 pantomime ended its run. It was always the custom there to give the children at least a brief glimpse of the Harlequinade, but it never happened until the pantomime had been running for a week or two.

On the first night Clown, at the end of the performance, would pop his head through the curtains and would greet the children with the promise that the Harlequinade would be seen later on. That was always rather a disappointment to young members of the audience. After that, when the pantomime had got into its swing, they would find room for a few minutes of the old-fashioned fun. And how the children used to enjoy it! And that enjoyment was not entirely confined to them, for many of the older playgoers in the audience, remembering the joys of their childhood, were delighted to see some of the ancient foolery again.

The disappearance of the Harlequinade and the banishment of Clown from the pantomime is to be regretted. Shall we never enjoy the fun of the red-hot poker again? Shall we never revel in Clown's delightful pranks upon the butcher and the baker, the swell and the policeman? Will no more geese and sausages be stolen? Shall we never again be thrilled by the slap of Harlequin's bat?

I am sad when I think it is several years since I saw even a ghost of a Harlequinade, but I haven't given up hope, although I searched the list of 1948 pantomimes in vain for any mention of a Clown.

But I found some encouragement when I saw *Cinderella* at the London Palladium, for during the show a troupe of Italian acrobatic dumb-show artists gave a delightful performance which the children seemed to enjoy more than anything else among the wonders. These performers, although wearing modern clothes, did everything that was once seen in the Harlequinade. They jumped through windows, darted through doors, dived down chimneys, disappeared through roofs, were chased by a policeman and went through all sorts of absurd antics. It was exactly the sort of thing that delighted the children of eighty years or more ago in the old-fashioned Harlequinade.

Perhaps one day some kind manager or producer of pantomime will be thoughtful enough to give our dear old friends of the Harlequinade a chance again. I should like to know what the Fairy Queen thinks about it. Has her magic wand lost its power? Can't she wave it once again and with some spell-commanding verse produce those beloved figures who used to appear at her bidding?

I like to think that Clown and his merry companions are only waiting in the wings ready to hear the joyous summons, at the sound of which and amid a blaze of red fire Joey will bound on with his old familiar greeting of "Here we are again!"

12

The Glories of Drury Lane

NO story of pantomime would be anything like correct if it did not give a great deal of credit to Drury Lane Theatre. That may surprise many of the younger generation who have never had an opportunity of seeing a Christmas show at what is sometimes known as the "National Theatre".

But at one time Drury Lane without a pantomime at Christmas-time was quite unthinkable. It was at this theatre that in the days of David Garrick some of the first pantomimes were staged. It was in Drury Lane pantomimes that some of the most popular artists became famous, and nearly every change in the form of this particular kind of entertainment seems to have had its origin there.

So perhaps it is not surprising that the theatre where the Harlequinade was once so popular should have been the first to deal so unkindly with Clown and to banish him from its boards.

But we mustn't think too unkindly of its famous manager, Sir Augustus Harris, who, because he encouraged the music-hall comedians to take the place of Clown and almost squeezed the Harlequinade out of the pantomime, was the first to deal the death-blow at an ancient institution. For it was he who raised the pantomime to a state of great magnificence with wonderful pageantry and he engaged the pick of artists and designers for his shows.

Drury Lane had had many ups-and-downs during its long existence. Theatres on its present site have been twice burnt down and managements have made and lost fortunes there. Just over a hundred years ago it went through a troublous time during which many different managers suffered losses.

There was a period during which a family of clever entertainers known as the Vokeses monopolised all the principal parts in its pantomimes. That began in 1869, and except for one year when the family went abroad it lasted for ten years.

Old Mr. Vokes was a theatrical costumier who carried on business near Drury Lane, so it was natural that his precociously clever children should take to the stage as they grew up. Most of them began by playing children's parts in Shakespearean plays.

The eldest of the family was Fred Vokes, who was such an expert dancer that he became known as "the man with the elastic legs". His sister Jessie took to the stage when she was only four, and one of those who taught her dancing was Flexmore, the Clown. There were two other sisters named Victoria and Rosina, and later on two other young men were "adopted" and were known was Fawdon and Walter Vokes. Their first appearance in pantomime was the Lyceum Theatre in 1868.

In *Aladdin*, the Drury Lane pantomime of 1874, they had all the best parts, for Fred Vokes was the wicked magician Abanazar, Fawdon was Kazrac, the dumb slave, Victoria was Aladdin, Rosina was the Princess, and Jessie the Genius of the Lamp. It was a real family affair, as you may see, and it was a great success, for Fred Vokes astounded everybody with his dancing. In 1875 they had all the principal parts in *Dick Whittington*, and on this occasion Walter was added to the cast as the Cat.

All these young people were enthusiastically admired at the time. Concerning "the marvellous legs" of Fred Vokes one writer said: "What speculations those legs suggest! Oh, if the schoolboy could only emulate some of their antics, what remarkable kicks he could accomplish at football, how he would paralyse the goalkeeper with laughter and what eccentric drops he would manage."

"Where in the world can we find their equal?" asked another enthusiast concerning Fred's surprising legs. "In them dancing is reduced to an art. They appear to be independent of his body, to fly about the stage by themselves and they play such fantastic tricks as would move any number of monks to mirth."

In time, however, the public began to tire of the dancing antics of the Vokes family, for very often they interfered with the fun and the efforts of the other performers. Their last appearance at Drury Lane was in *Cinderella* in 1879, and during the run of that unfortunate pantomime the theatre was suddenly closed. As the Vokes family had not received their salaries, they refused to perform, so there was nothing for the poor manager to do but to shut down.

This failure provided the great opportunity to the twenty-eight-year old Augustus Harris, who, though little more than a youth, took over the management of the theatre. He was the youngest man who had ever had control of London's leading theatre.

For sixteen years or so he presented pantomimes more gorgeous and elaborate than London had ever experienced and he introduced the best possible talent. It was he who discovered the peculiar comic genius of Dan Leno and, providing Herbert Campbell as his partner, presented the most popular pantomime pair ever known.

Augustus Harris's first pantomime was *Bluebeard*. It was the first time that the story had been presented at Drury Lane, and the Vokes family were engaged for all the principal parts. It was their last engagement there, however, for Harris had already made up his mind to dispense with them. He resented what he had come to regard as a tyrannical monopoly and thought the Vokes' family had long outstayed its welcome. In later pantomimes he engaged such popular comedians as James Fawn and Arthur Roberts and they helped to develop the drastic change from the old type of performance.

No one suffered more from this change and more resented it than poor Mr. Blanchard, who had been writing the pantomimes for Drury Lane regularly since 1852. He had a poetic vein in his nature and his taste was all for the simple and fairy-like story that would certainly appeal to children, if not to all grown-ups. Naturally, therefore, he was quite out of sympathy with the style of pantomime which Harris was developing, and we know what this kindly, gentle man must have suffered in seeing his work tampered with and – in his opinion – vulgarised and coarsened by the introduction of music-hall humour. We know this because his diaries were published after his death and they disclose some quite touching passages. Here, for instance, is what he wrote in November 1881:

"Sketching out second scene in pantomime by midnight, not pleasant work as it used to be owing to the terrible but, I fear, profitable music-hall innovations introduced in it."

Later on he wrote:

"Hardly anything done as I intended it, or spoken as I had written; the music-hall element is crushing out the rest and the good old fairy-tales never again to be illustrated as they should be."

After he had seen *Aladdin* in 1885 he wrote even more pathetically:

"It is more dazzling than funny, and I get very weary of the gagging of the music-hall people and with eyes dazzled with gas and glitter cannot stay till midnight when the Harlequinade only commences and which few now care about. Oh, the change from one's boyhood! left to be rattled through as rapidly as possible and without I fear, any adequate rehearsal."

The last pantomime to which the name of poor Mr. Blanchard was attached was *The Babes in the Wood* in 1888, but little of what he had written had been allowed to remain. The entry in his diary, written shortly before his death, in which he said "My smooth and pointed lines are turned into ragged prose and arrant nonsense", is the saddest thing that this good writer of such pleasant fancy ever recorded.

I do not think that full justice has ever been done to the memory of Mr. Blanchard, whose pantomimes delighted children for so many generations, not only at Drury Lane, but at many other theatres in London and the provinces.

His life was one of hard toil – for apart from writing pantomimes he was a very busy journalist – and of sacrifice for others. Though he never earnt a great deal of money, he was generous in support of the needy members of his family and he was surprisingly patient with them.

He enjoyed writing his pantomimes (which he always referred to as "annuals") and put all his best work into them. His verses, as I hope I have shown, are full of graceful and charming fancy as well as of playful humour, and he treated nursery-legends, fairy-tales and familiar stories in a way that particularly appealed to children, of whom he had great understanding. He could take the simplest of nursery rhymes and turn it into an ingenious and pleasing story, and he always kept alive the fairy element and the atmosphere of wonderment and magic without which a really good pantomime is quite incomplete.

He was a great loss to the spirit of make-believe, and in that respect I think he deserves to be out on an equality with that other gentle writer of fairy-lore – the Danish Hans Christian Andersen, with whom, I am sure, he would have found much in common.

In Denmark there are monuments and other memorials to remind children of what they owe to their great national story-teller, but here there is no memorial to the good Mr. Blanchard, who did so much to entertain British children with the creations of his kindly fancy. It is a pity that so much of what he wrote has died with him, but from his now forgotten pantomimes I have tried to extract some examples of his pleasant rhymes and couplets; enough to show, I hope, that his name deserves to be remembered with gratitude and admiration.

And now I must return to Sir Augustus Harris, who, although he took trouble enough to engage leading comedians for his pantomimes, never really worried much about the comic part. That was a matter which he was content to leave to the invention of the comedians themselves. What he was much concerned with was the pageantry and splendour

– magnificent scenery, gorgeous tableaux and, above all, imposing processions that often filled the vast stage of Drury Lane Theatre with armies of marching men, women and children clad in dazzling finery.

He had a great contempt for the old style of pantomime. He once said: "A popular Clown with a veteran to assist him as Pantaloon, one of the ballet gentlemen from the Opera House dressed like Harlequin and one of the first row of the ballet as Columbine were supposed to be enough to attract our forefathers to the pantomime."

He was never at a loss for an excuse to introduce a procession. In one pantomime there would be a gorgeous parade of "remarkable women of all ages" from Semiramis, Queen of Babylon, to Napoleon's Josephine. In another there was a procession representing the heroines of Shakespeare's plays. Yet another introduced representatives of England's world-wide possessions, beginning with the annexation of India and ending with a general tribute to Britain from her numerous colonies and dependencies.

On one occasion there was an unending parade representing twenty-one English sports; on another a procession introducing all the Kings and Queens of England, with their Courts and attendants. For this display (which must have given the children the idea that instead of being entertained by pantomime fun they were being given a history lesson) Sir Augustus had consulted every learned authority in order that the detail might be correct, for he was always insistent upon strict accuracy.

There was a procession representing twenty-four different nations one Christmastide. There were Tartar maidens in amber silk and furs, girls from Cochin China in creamy robes and feathered headdresses, Lapps in white furs, Japanese in embroidered purple, girls from China in terracotta and gold robes, Greek damsels in classic draperies, Spanish señoritas in black lace mantillas, Americans in Stars and Stripes – all this to introduce the famous Marie Lloyd as Princess Allfair in bridal array.

In *Ali Baba and the Forty Thieves* the stage was filled with three or four hundred people representing the invasion of the robbers' den. Each of the forty thieves was accompanied by a train of ten or twelve people! It is said that all this kind of thing, however, gorgeous and dazzling and expensive, bored the children, who were inclined to be restless as the processions wended their long way and to wonder how long it would be before the fun was resumed. I must certainly say that I sympathise with this point of view, for I remember my own agonies of boredom as a child when there was too much pageantry on the stage.

Sometimes, as these processions unwound themselves, there were hitches and disasters to prolong the business. On one occasion during the performance of *Sinbad the Sailor* in 1882 everything went wrong. The scenery was very beautiful, but it would keep sticking. A gigantic roc had been constructed for the valley scene. It was made large enough to lift up Sinbad, but it stuck fast on Boxing Night, and in spite of all the efforts of the stage hands it could not be removed to make way for the next scene.

However, I won't dwell upon Sir Augustus Harris's occasional failures. Let us look rather at some of his successes, and they were plentiful enough, by all accounts. "On the stage commanded by Augustus Harris the tales of Fairyland are annually illustrated with a magnificence which sets criticism at naught," said a writer one year. "They hardly fall within the domain of drama. They are a dream, a phantasmagoria, the baseless fabric of a vision and are best approached in a spirit of childlike wonderment."

Here is a description of a "Dismal Swamp" scene which came towards the end of *Aladdin*:

"In truth it is a dismal place. Monstrous creatures crawl about in it; great bats flap their lazy wings. The Demon who owns the freehold of this undesirable site and who appears as a gigantic frog, is disinclined to part with his rights. He has therefore to be fought and overcome by another demon and a tremendous combat ensues, the rival demons appearing and disappearing through traps with lightning speed. In the end the demon frog is vanquished and Aladdin is free to proceed with his palatial schemes.

"A further rub of the magic lamp changes the swamp into a fertile plain with a lake in the background. Myriads of tiny British workmen troop in and, having erected a hoarding with the strange device 'Gusarris, Builder and Decorator', proceed to build a palace behind it. When the scaffolding is removed is seen a beautiful palace with a practicable bridge which provides a picturesque route for the brilliant procession of Aladdin's retainers."

I should like to give you a picture of one of Sir Augustus Harris's famous Boxing Night productions at Drury Lane. It is a description of the first performance of *Mother Goose and the Enchanted Beauty* in 1880 written by Clement Scott.

"Mother Goose and the Enchanted Beauty – what a capital title," he wrote. "This excellent old creature who little children will be delighted to hear lives in 'Lowther Arcadia'* is opposed in the orthodox fashion to the spiteful witch Malignia, and they fight incontinently over the life and destiny of the pretty princess. When that silly old Lord Chamberlain forgot to invite the witch Malignia to the christening he little thought what confusion he would create at the christening, for the old woman vows vengeance against the child and declares she shall die before she comes of age, injured by a spindle. A decree goes out in the story-book fashion, to banish all spindles from the realm; but, dear me, on the very eve of her majority the Princess hocusses her waiting-maids with rum in their afternoon tea and falls a victim to the snares of Malignia in disguise. She is injured by a spindle as fate decreed, but good old Mother Goose declares she shall not die, but sleep for a hundred years and wake as young as ever, kissed by a handsome young prince.

"Away goes the story on the track of the Sleeping Prin-

* Lowther Arcade, which once stood in the Strand, was notable for its toy shops.—AUTHOR.

DAN LENO AS A DRURY LANE DAME

A PRINCIPAL BOY OF 1903: BIRDIE SUTHERLAND

GEORGE GRAVES AS A DAME

HERBERT CAMPBELL AT DRURY LANE, 1900

cess and further opportunities are given for sylvan scenery, enchanting glades, and a moving panorama that will for its ingenuity and charm be the talk of London. . . . The Court awakes from its slumbers, not young but hideously old! That all comes from not consulting Mother Goose, who, however, has an instant remedy in her golden eggs that can rejuvenate an assembled Court and make them beautiful for ever. . . . What a wonderful pantomime with its ballet of joys, its mythical ballet describing 'the flight of one thousand years', its sylvan groves and pastoral haunts of Arcadian shepherds and shepherdesses, its demon-haunted wood and moving panorama, its sleeping Court and upheaval of awakening until that delightful turn when the curtain falls and good little boys and girls can believe that the end was accomplished by the magic wand of the author and can hear the fairy Princess saying as they fall to sleep:

> Oh, seek my father's court with me,
> For there are greater wonders there;
> And o'er the hills and far away,
> Beyond the utmost purple rim
> Beyond the night across the sky;
> Through all the world they followed him."

That will give an idea of Blanchard's ingenuity in combining two well-known nursery legends into one delightful story. It must have been an enchanting pantomime.

Managers of other theatres began to copy Sir Augustus Harris's partiality for processions and pageantry. Looking over the provincial pantomimes in 1886, a writer found that the tendency to produce an elaborate spectacle instead of a bustling, funny pantomime was on the increase. "Laughter is sacrificed for scenery and general dullness is the result of a too ambitious motive to please the eye," he complained.

Much about the same time an old playgoer wrote "Little by little the modest requirements which had for so long satisfied our forefathers have been entirely thrown in the shade owing to the increasing mania for spectacular magnificence and scenic display. . . . That the result is 'ultra-gorgeous' it is impossible to deny; but as far as amusement goes it may be doubted if we have gained by the change."

It must be admitted that Sir Augustus Harris often put too much magnificence into his pantomimes, but on the other hand it was he who, with Dan Leno and Herbert Campbell, gave pantomime the finest combination of comedians it has ever known – but that is a story which deserves a chapter to itself.

13

The Story of Dan Leno

THE name of Dan Leno, like that of John Rich and Joseph Grimaldi, will for ever be linked with that of pantomime. He is one of the few immortals of the traditional Christmas entertainment. No one ever adorned the world of topsy-turvy make-believe more naturally than he. No one ever raised the comic part of it to such a height of perfection, nor has any other comedian adorned it with a quainter collection of humorous portraits – grotesque "dames", odd queens, quaint monarchs, all delightful in their drollery.

Sir Augustus Harris is generally credited with the "discovery" of Leno as a pantomime comedian, but actually it was George Conquest of the Surrey Theatre who first saw in the variety comedian and champion clog-dancer the possibilities of a pantomime artist.

Like so many of his kind Leno (whose real name was Galvin) was born of poor parentage and had a hard upbringing. He was born in Somers Town, a shabby quarter of London, and his father and mother were music-hall performers. As a youth he became a skilful clog-dancer and in that way earned his living in the cheaper kind of music halls. He made his first appearance in London at a music hall in the East End. George Conquest went there and heard him singing "Fetching in the Milk for the Twins", and was so struck by his quaint manner that he engaged him and his wife to appear in the Surrey Theatre pantomime of 1886 at a joint salary of £20 a week. There Dan played the "dame".

Such was his success that he was engaged as principal comedian in *Sinbad the Sailor* for the following year.

As a young man he had set his heart on appearing at Drury Lane. It was the natural ambition of any comedian. His cousin and life-long friend, Johnny Danvers with whom

99

he often acted, once said to him: "Dan, I've often heard you say you have never seen 'the Lane'. Let's walk over and have a look at the outside now."

They walked over to the famous old theatre and paused before its portico entrance. After looking at it for a few minutes in silence Dan, to the surprise of his companion, walked up the steps and knelt on the topmost one. Then rising and returning he took Johnny Danvers by the arm and said quietly: "Johnny, I shall act there some day."

And so it happened. Sir Augustus Harris saw him when he played Tinbad the Tailor in *Sinbad the Sailor* and engaged him to appear in *The Babes in the Wood*, the Drury Lane pantomime of 1888, at a salary of £28 a week. His part was only a small one, for the principal comedians were Harry Nicholls and Herbert Campbell, who was to become his great friend and partner in many Christmas pantomimes.

I have previously mentioned this particular pantomime, but let me now give you a picture of the babes as they appeared to George Augustus Sala.

"Very rarely indeed", he wrote, "have these two admirable drolls been seen to greater advantage. Their costumes and make-up were, to begin with, almost beyond praise. Mr. Nicholls in a yoked muslin frock, pink legs, frills and socks looked like Alice in Wonderland seen in a grotesquely distorting looking-glass; Mr. Campbell in knickerbockers, a broad sash and fair hair irresistibly suggested Little Lord Fauntleroy writ large.

"How they made their first appearance holding a doll between them; how Bertie sucked a stick of barley sugar while Cissie sucked her thumb; how they always appeared side by side 'like twin cherries on one stalk' in a perambulator out of which, of course, by dint of mutual nudging and slapping they fell; how they rebelled at having their faces washed by the nursery governess and how they wandered into the wood with the two robbers and by dint of artlessness and ignorance moved those ferocious marauders to compassion, and how as a culmination of their efforts Messrs. Harry Nicholls and Herbert Campbell appeared in the scene of the Paradise of Birds in full ballet costume, Cissie in skirts of verdant hue and Bertie as Cupid God of Love, bow and arrow and all, and danced a *pas de deux* to the almost delirious delight of the house, are feats of humour and agility which we have not space to describe in detail, but which must be seen to be fully appreciated."

In *Jack and the Beanstalk*, the pantomime of the following year, Dan Leno appeared as Mrs. Simpson, Jack's fond mother. In 1891 he and Herbert Campbell became partners for the first time in *Humpty Dumpty*. They were a perfect contrast, for Leno was small, mercurial and lively, while Campbell was big, solid and smilingly amiable.

Dan Leno was always at his best when he was playing dame parts. His short stature, his whimsical, surprised and eager look, his odd manner of dressing up, made him a very comical figure. Even if he had been silent you would have laughed at him.

One of his biggest successes was in *Mother Goose* in 1902, when, it is written, "He made a comical entrance as a humble widow seated in a little country cart alongside a crate containing live geese and peacefully driving a pair of donkeys along a country lane. As the cavalcade reached the cross roads a motor horn was heard and a car driven by a huge gentleman enveloped in furs dashed into the little country cart.

"Over went the cart and there ensued a scene of the wildest confusion amid which one had visions of Leno in all parts of the stage at once, Leno raising the struggling donkeys to their feet, Leno rescuing geese that had escaped from the crate and finally Leno grasping by the neck an excited and struggling goose in either hand and alternately slanging the chauffeur in English, French and German."

Dan Leno was comical enough in this kind of thing, but it was when he was taking the audience into his confidence and telling them odd things about his (or her) domestic life and family troubles that he was particularly amusing – at least, that is to say, to the grown-ups, though perhaps the point of what he had to say could not always be so readily understood by younger members of the audience. They preferred him, I dare say, when he performed his amusing antics or when he sang or danced.

But when in his comical get-up as an elderly woman – a little wizened figure with screwed-up hair, high, arched eyebrows and an eager and friendly look – he would advance to the footlights and address the audience with the air of being among a circle of intimate friends the grown-ups would shriek with laughter over his woes and his queer observations. This kind of humour does not, of course, look quite so funny in cold print as when Dan Leno would utter it in his eager, excited way and in that dry husky tone that carried to the furthest part of the house. But let me give you a small sample. This is what he had to say as Mrs. Twankay, Aladdin's mother, as she was hanging out the washing in her laundry back garden:

"Oh dear! What is there about washing that makes people so bad-tempered? I'm sorry I ever adopted it as a profession. But there, when Mustapha left me to battle with an untrusting world what could I do? I tried lady barbering, but the customers were too attentive and I – poor simple child – was full of unsophisticatedness and I believed their honeyed words. I remember young Lord Plumpler agitated me so with his badinage that there was a slight accident. I believe he would have proposed to me, but in my confusion I cut the end of his nose off. Ah! it was a near shave.

"Then I went on the stage as Juliet. Oh, the bouquets they threw at me! Not silly useless hot-house flowers, but cauliflowers and garden fruit like that. When they repaired the theatre I asked for a re-engagement, but the manager was out. Then I had an idea. All Society ladies were learning to be useful in dressmaking, millinery, painting and journalism. So I founded this select laundry for the daughters of decayed noblemen. It was all right at first, but I soon found that as my pupils left me my trade decreased – every lady became her own laundress. Never mind; the weather forecast says it will rain in Brixton, so there may be a storm in Hackney. Then, if it rains, we shall have water and business will look up."

Then there were the arguments he would have with one of his stage partners. There was a very funny scene in *Blue Beard* when he appeared as Sister Anne. As Blue Beard, Herbert Campbell announced his intention of going in for travel, so they decided to look up suitable trains in "Bradshaw's Guide". Then this dialogue took place:

ANNE. Where are you going?

BLUE BEARD. I'm going to a place called Puzzleton.

ANNE. Puzzleton? How do you get there?

BLUE BEARD. That's what I'm trying to find out. Here you are. There's a train at 9.40 marked B. What does that mean?

ANNE. B? Cattle only.

BLUE BEARD. That's no good.

ANNE. There's one at 10.30 marked J. See what J means.

BLUE BEARD. J – see page 406.

ANNE. There it is – "J – see page 108."

BLUE BEARD. Why, that's where we started from.

ANNE. So it is. What silly things guides are.

BLUE BEARD. Here you are, J – I've got it, 10.30 train to Puzzleton. "This train runs on Sundays, Wednesdays and Fridays only during September and July, except on the 15th of each month, then it runs on Tuesday and on Thursday and Saturday from the 9th of June to the 8th of August, except on Bank holidays and Sundays, when it starts at 6.50. On all other occasions it runs as usual."

ANNE. That's a very good train.

BLUE BEARD. Yes, but I don't think I'll go by it.

ANNE. Let me see. I understand these things. Look here! You start by the 11.30 express; that takes you to the edge of the desert in time to catch the 2.30 camel; the camel brings you across the desert to Tra-ra-ra Junction, where you meet the 5.16 elephant that brings you to the 9.20 steamer.

BLUE BEARD. That isn't a steamer; it's a balloon.

ANNE. So it is. Well! The 9.20 balloon brings you as far as Muddle Circus, where you take the blue bus with the umbrella over the driver. See? Look for yourself.

BLUE BEARD. 11.30 express. Here we are. Z – what's that? Z – Shrove Tuesday and Christmas Day only.

No wonder that after much more of that headaching sort of thing they ended the discussion by breaking into a song and dance.

Then there was another amusing scene in *Humpty Dumpty*, when Dan Leno was the Queen and Harry Randall the Royal cook. The Queen went into the Royal kitchen on a mission of inquiry and this is what was heard:

QUEEN. I want to talk to you about those tradesmen's bills. Really the extravagance that goes on in this kitchen is terrible. (*She produces bills.*)
COOK. There's nothing wasted here, I assure you.
QUEEN (*pointing to item*). One onion, threepence.
COOK. That's right. It's a wholesome fruit.
QUEEN. But see here again, lower down, one onion threepence.
COOK. Yes, that's the same onion.
QUEEN. Then here's the butcher's bill. How much a pound do you give for steak?
COOK. It all depends – from one-and-twopence to tenpence.
QUEEN. What kind of steaks do you get for tenpence?
COOK. Engine steaks.
QUEEN. Engine steaks – what are they?
COOK. Not tender.
QUEEN. Ah, now I see your loco-motive.
COOK. What shall I send up for lunch today?
QUEEN. I was coming to that. I think I will have the cold beef.
COOK. Cold beef?
QUEEN. Yes, you know, the piece we roasted yesterday.
COOK. Oh, I never thought you'd want to see *that* little bit again.
QUEEN. Little *bit*? It was a great big joint yesterday.

The cook replies that it wasn't worth serving up and that she gave it to the cat. She blames the cat also for the disappearance of other articles of food, including fish, pickled pork and a brace of pheasants. Finally the Queen says sarcastically, in reference to some other missing dish: "You gave it to the cat?" "I gave it to the cat," says the Cook. "Same cat?" asks the Queen. "Same cat," replies the Cook. "Then serve the cat up for lunch" demands the Queen as she leaves the kitchen.

The foregoing extracts may give you an idea of the kind of fun they had year after year in Drury Lane pantomimes. There was always some hilarious scene in which

Dan Leno took prominent part. In *The Forty Thieves* he was Abdullah and there was glorious fun when he and Herbert Campbell as Fatima, being in need of money, broke into a building which looked like a bank, but turned out to be Newgate Prison. In *Blue Beard* Leno sang ballads to his own harp accompaniment and finished up by getting dreadfully entangled in the strings of the instrument, after which he played ping-pong with a frying-pan and potatoes in the kitchen.

In *Humpty Dumpty* he and Harry Randall sat under the Tree of Truth, which, every time one or other of them told a fib, dropped fruit on their heads. It ended in quite a shower.

Yes, Dan Leno was the life and soul of fun and one of the most popular favourites ever to appear in pantomime. The public loved that droll little figure with the husky voice and strangely appealing manner in which there was always a touch of wistfulness. "Surely among Britons there never lived a more universal favourite than he," wrote the author of his biography. "He did not appeal to any class or section. He appealed to all, from the King to his humblest subject."

Dan Leno had indeed appeared before the King, who had presented him with a diamond pin. After that he was always referred to as "the King's Jester", and you can guess how proud the little comedian was of that title.

But there was tragedy in store for this supreme fun-maker. He became very ill in 1902 and for a time was confined in a private mental institution, but he was able to appear in the pantomime at Christmas. His condition grew serious again the following summer, although he recovered sufficiently to appear in another pantomime at Christmas. It was *Humpty Dumpty*. There had been much public anxiety about his health, and so when after several months' absence from the stage he reappeared at Drury Lane on Boxing Night 1903 he had a wonderful reception. The audience rejoiced to see that comical, wistful little figure again and they nearly raised the roof of the theatre with their applause.

He played on that occasion with all his old familiar humour; in fact, it was one of his best performances. During the pantomime he and his customary partner Herbert Campbell had a duet with the refrain:

> And we hope to appear
> For many a year
> In the panto of old Drury Lane.

How sad it is to know that within a few months both these merry men were dead.

Herbert Campbell died as the result of an accident on July 19, 1904, and Dan Leno, grief for his old friend and partner aggravating his ailment, followed him in the autumn. He was only forty-three years of age. It was one of the greatest losses that pantomime has ever suffered.

How right it was of one newspaper to say of him: "Mr. Leno not only had a rich fund of comedy in his own quaint face and personality; but had that far rarer gift – the intelligence to make use of it. . . . He had imagination. He was not content to trade solely on what nature had given him. He could hardly walk and certainly never danced without raising a smile."

This was only one of the many tributes paid to the comic genius of a kindly and delightful artist.

"He excelled all other music-hall comedians in intelligence, drollery and creativeness," wrote E. V. Lucas. "Leno's long series of largely irresponsible but always human pantomime figures differed from all pantomime figures by their strange blend of fun and wistfulness."

"It needs no courage or jugglery of speech to say that Dan Leno was a genius," wrote Wilfred Whitten. "Let anyone call up the scene and atmosphere of one of his performances, and then shut his eyes and remember and compare, and he will see that Dan Leno brought something to the stage that was not in his song or in his talk, or anything of his nameable qualities; not even in his humour. None of these really distinguished him from the other. Behind all lay a unique quality to which one cannot put a word."

But one of the loveliest tributes to his quality, capturing the very essence of his appeal, was written by Max Beerbohm.

"The moment that Dan Leno skipped upon the stage", he wrote, "we were aware that here was a man utterly unlike anyone else we had seen. . . . I defy anyone not to have loved Dan Leno at first sight. The moment he capered on, with that air of wild determination, squirming in every limb with some deep grievance that must be outpoured, all hearts were his. That face puckered with cares, whether they were the cares of the small shopkeeper or the landlady, or of the lodger; that face so tragic, with all the tragedy that is writ on the face of a baby-monkey, yet ever liable to relax its mouth into a sudden wide grin and to screw up its eyes to vanishing-point over some little triumph wrested from Fate, the tyrant; that poor little battered personage, so 'put upon' yet so plucky, with his squeaking voice and his sweeping gestures; bent but not broken; faint but pursuing; incarnate of the will to live in a world not at all worth living in – surely all hearts went out to Dan Leno, with warm corners in them reserved to him for ever and ever."

14

A Great Pantomime Writer

WHEN Sir Augustus Harris died in 1896 opportunity to control the fortunes of Drury Lane Theatre and the future of pantomime came to another enterprising young man named Arthur Collins, who was responsible for nearly all the subsequent Christmas productions there until the annual custom was at last regrettably broken.

Arthur Collins certainly did much to alter and improve pantomime in many ways. Under his direction they were all very fine and elaborate entertainments and in the opinion of many people they have never been surpassed. However, there have been a few who considered that he did a good deal of harm to the Christmas entertainment. For instance, Alfred Lane Crauford, who was for a long time manager of a rival home of pantomime, the Britannia Theatre, Hoxton, once told me: "Perhaps no man did so much harm to pantomime as Arthur Collins. He it was who cut out the glories of the transformation scene and substituted for it a gorgeous procession. Thereby the pantomime was cut into two parts. Formerly the curtain never fell.

"The final blow to the old 'comic scenes' was given by Collins. Harry Payne used to be given about ten minutes and practically all he did was to throw bon-bons to the audience. The other theatres of London and the provinces were influenced by Drury Lane. They went in for processions, cut out the transformation scene, and made only a pretence at the comic scenes."

But Collins certainly did many good things for pantomime, and if he had a definite fault it was that he was always inclined to give the theatregoer too much for his money. Perhaps you don't agree that that is a fault and that you can have too much pantomime in one evening. I know that some years ago when I took one of my sons to the dress-rehearsal of a pantomime at the Adelphi Theatre which lasted for about six hours his only grumble was that it ended too early! But that, I'm afraid, is not the opinion of most grown-up pantomime-goers, and very often they grew impatient with the pantomimes of Arthur Collins, which sometimes lasted as long as five hours.

Though he went in for extravagant costumes, masses of performers, beautiful scenery and other expensive things, he was not so keen on pageantry and unending processions as Sir Augustus Harris had been. And I think, too, he had the right idea of adding more humour to the performances.

It must be regretted that, like Sir Augustus, he had little love for the old-fashioned Harlequinade. As the funny business developed the opportunities for Clown and Co. dwindled into almost nothing and finally vanished completely. It was he, too, I think, who abolished the other old-fashioned business of the Demon King or other unpleasant spirit, in darting up through trap-doors. He considered that that sort of thing frightened the children.

When Dan Leno and Herbert Campbell died Mr. Collins had to look round for some other comedians for his pantomimes. He found many, though none of them ever quite filled the places of those beloved favourites.

One of the first of them was Harry Randall, who was always very diverting as a "dame". "We would say of him as of another famous character that his face is his fortune," said *The Times* on one occasion: "a variegated face, an india-rubber face, the whole Mercator's Projection of a face – if it were not for his agreeable (or at any rate not disagreeable) strident voice and his extremely eloquent, versatile and vivacious legs."

Then came Fred Emney, Wilkie Bard, who used to introduce such tongue-twisting songs as "She Sells Sea-shells on the Seashore", and that very amusing comedian George Graves, whose ripe and slangy humour echoing the chatter of the smoking-room and the Turf, however, perhaps always appealed more to the grown-ups than to the youngsters, despite his comical appearance.

In *Aladdin* he was a particularly droll Abanazar, especially when he carried live fowls and a barrel-organ among his luggage in an airship. He was delightful again as a king who had lost his memory in *Hop o' My Thumb*, which introduced a child actress named Renée Meyer who was quite an enchanting little hero.

I like to remember George Graves best as the unfortunate Duke of Monte Blanco in *The Sleeping Beauty*. In this pantomime the Wicked Fairy turned him into a scarecrow. There for years he remained suspended by the roadside. Mice had built their nests in his pockets, mushrooms grew from his toes, and a golf ball from an adjoining course had stuck in his ear. It was delightful to see him awakening from his long sleep, shaking the birds' nests from his ragged clothing and stretching his stiff and aching limbs.

He had as his partner that very droll comedian Will Evans, whose father, Fred Evans, by the way, was a popular Clown who played in the pantomimes in the good old days of the Harlequinade at Drury Lane. Graves and Evans had a very funny scene in a photographic dark-room where they were much puzzled over the mysteries of developing a picture, and there was a rollicking scene, too, when they ventured upon paperhanging.

During his rule of Drury Lane, Arthur Collins decided to defy one of the conventions of pantomime by engaging a man to play the part of "principal boy" instead of employing some shapely young woman. That happened in 1912, in *The Sleeping Beauty*, when the part of Prince Auriol was performed by a well-known singer named Wilfrid Douthitt, in *The Sleeping Beauty Beautified*, when Bertram Wallis was the hero, and in *Puss in Boots*, when Eric Marshall was the Prince. But when the latter pantomime was repeated in 1916 the first World War was raging and there was other work for men to do, so Mr. Collins went back to the old tradition. Since then, alas! there have been very few principal boys of either kind at Drury Lane, for in 1920 there was no pantomime for the first time in nearly seventy years. It marked the beginning of the end of Drury Lane as the great national home of pantomime.

This happened because a highly successful drama was running at the theatre and it did not seem wise to take it off to make room for pantomime. Instead *Cinderella*, which had been extremely successful during the previous year, was performed at Covent Garden Theatre. In 1921 the theatre was closed for reconstruction, and Arthur Collins having died, there was no pantomime again until *The Sleeping Beauty* in 1929. Since then there have been only two other pantomimes.

So the long tradition of Drury Lane pantomime may now be regarded as ended. The costs of producing a play on the large stage of the theatre are so great in these days that it does not pay a management to remove a successful production merely in order to make way for a Christmas show. The end of a great tradition, associated with so many famous people, must have grieved many old playgoers to whom the idea of Boxing Night without a journey to see the fun of Drury Lane and all the attendant excitements among an eager audience would at one time have been almost unthinkable.

Before leaving the subject of Drury Lane Theatre I should say something about a man who did much to raise the standard of pantomime writing, a man who stood above his rivals as high as did E. L. Blanchard in his day. In fact, I doubt if better pantomimes in modern times have ever been written than those of J. Hickory Wood, and probably no man in his particular line was ever more financially successful. Though he died in 1913, the pantomimes that he wrote especially for Drury Lane are still played every Christmas at many theatres up and down the country. In one year during his lifetime (1911) no fewer than thirty-three of his pantomimes were running simultaneously in England, South Africa, and Australia.

His real name was John James Wood and he was originally a Manchester insurance agent. He took to song-writing
after an accidental meeting during a summer holiday with a
well-known entertainer who complained that he couldn't
find the right kind of song lyric. So Wood wrote something
for him and the entertainer was so delighted that he was
kept busily employed in writing other material.

He soon became well known in the theatrical world, and
when towards the end of 1900 Arthur Collins, disappointed
by another writer, was in need of an author for the next
Drury Lane pantomime he got into touch with Wood, who
wrote *Blue Beard* for him. Collins was delighted with his
work and Wood became the regular writer for Drury Lane.

The best of his productions was *Mother Goose*, and it is
highly probable that many of my readers may have seen it
on the stage, for it has been in constant use ever since it
was written. It may not be generally known that the present-
day version was his own invention. All that was originally
known concerning the legend of Mother Goose was that
she was associated with a goose that laid golden eggs. That
was all that Wood had to go upon when he came to write
the pantomime. So he invented a charming story in which
Mother Goose is a poor woman who is used to illustrate the
moral that riches do not always bring happiness and con-
tentment. The good and bad fairies agree to put the matter
to the test by sending Mother Goose the goose that lays
the golden eggs. At the first sign of discontent the goose
will fly away.

The goose brings the old lady riches, but that does not
exactly satisfy her, because, despite the good fairy's warning,
she wishes to become beautiful. She obtains her desire by
bathing in a magic pool, but then she finds that despite her
newly-acquired beauty nobody wants her. She is consequently discontented, and so the goose flies away. However, Mother Goose has a good friend in Colin, her daughter's sweetheart. He regains the goose; Mother Goose is
content to lose her beauty and all live happy ever after.

PANTOMIME AS IT IS: FITZWARREN'S STORES IN TOM ARNOLD'S "DICK WHITTINGTON"

A MODERN PANTOMIME SETTING: DICK WHITTINGTON'S DREAM IN A TOM ARNOLD PRODUCTION

That is the story that Hickory Wood invented. It is an excellent one and much better than the version of the legend in which Joseph Grimaldi figured. Those who have seen that excellent comedian, George Lacey, perform the leading part will have some idea of the comedy that it once provided for Dan Leno, for whom the part was originally written.

Hickory Wood was not only skilful in adapting the old, familiar fairy-tales and in inventing new situations without spoiling the original outline, but he had the particular ability of writing dialogue that exactly fitted the peculiar styles of the comedians. It had become the custom for many pantomime-writers to leave that sort of thing to the comedians themselves. Not so with Hickory Wood. The dialogue and the jokes which he supplied for Dan Leno and Herbert Campbell might have been their own invention so precisely were they characteristic of their individual styles and personalities.

He was also a graceful writer of rhyme. Here, for example, is a typical passage from the opening scene in *Sleeping Beauty and the Beast*, when the Fairy Queen, making her entry in the Fairies' Bower says:

> What do I see? My Fairyland at play?
> What of the work you've always loved to do?
> This is a holiday, but not for you.
> The people on the earth whom we befriend
> Await those Christmas presents that we send:
> The dolls, the crackers, wooden horses, sweets,
> The toys, the boxes of paints that baby eats.
> You must not let this work go to the wall,
> So go and do it.
>
> FAIRY. Please, we've done it all.
> FAIRY QUEEN. 'Tis mortals who cease work at set of sun;
> But fairy's work, you know, is never done.
> There live on earth a worthy king and queen,
> Who, though their married life has happy been,
> Are yet without a child to call their own
> On which account they've melancholy grown.
> Suppose a little child we hide away,

H

In parsley bed, for them to find today.
ALL. Oh yes, we will!
FAIRY QUEEN. And yes we will, say I.
We'll send them down a present from the sky.
And here she is, a little daughter fair,
The fairies' gift unto the royal pair.

Then in the pretty scene in the Palace of Sleep the Fairy
Queen is made to say:

While Beauty's slept, the days have swiftly flown
And each one has an int'rest of its own.
The spring brings forth the tender valentine,
And then the yellow primrose is the sign
That Easter-tide draws near, to pave the way
For blossoms sweet to crown the Queen of May.
Then summer brings her roses white and red,
When rosy petals bloom, and none are shed
When, in the meadow 'mid the new-mown hay,
Are men at work, while happy children play
Till Autumn when the harvest's safe in store
And sportsmen in the stubble range once more,
While leaves are falling thick and fast
To show the year will soon be of the past
Yet, ere it dies, does each succeeding year
Bring Father Christmas and his ancient cheer.
To Beauty in her dream I wish to show,
How year by year the swift days come and go.

Perhaps I might mention in concluding this chapter about
Drury Lane Theatre that it was J. Hickory Wood who wrote
the very interesting and understanding life-story of his great
friend, Dan Leno.

15

Drury Lane's Rivals

IN this history of pantomime I have said a good deal about Drury Lane Theatre, but as will be gathered from my references to other London theatres it was not by any means the only theatre that regularly provided the seasonable Christmas entertainment, nor was it the first of the theatres to be associated with the stage performances of Clown, Harlequin and of fairy-lore.

At one period Drury Lane had more than half a dozen rivals. Just to give you an idea of how pantomime once flourished in the principal theatres I can tell you that if you had been a child seventy years or so ago you could have had your choice between *Aladdin* at Drury Lane, *The Babes in the Wood* at Covent Garden, *Children in the Wood* at the Adelphi, *Beauty and the Beast* at the Princess's, *Sinbad* at the Holborn, *Robinson Crusoe* at the Standard, *The Forty Thieves* at the Surrey, *Jack and Jill* at the Victoria, *Aladdin; or, Harlequin and the Flying Horses of Lambeth* at Astley's, to say nothing of such jolly entertainments as they had at the Britannia and the Grecian Theatres. At no period, in fact, was pantomime ever quite so popular.

Of all those theatres Covent Garden was Drury Lane's closest rival. The original theatre on this site was specially built for John Rich in 1732, and until the year 1887 it was regularly the home of the best kind of pantomime. Since that year, however, the theatre has been devoted mostly to opera and ballet and has staged pantomime on only two occasions.

Many of the theatres I have mentioned have long since vanished and others have remained only as pathetic ghosts of brick and mortar. Let me tell you something about them.

There never was a theatre more remarkable than the Britannia at Hoxton, which in its day was affectionately known as the "old Brit". Although the theatre was hidden away in one of the poorest and dingiest quarters of London, it drew audiences for its pantomimes from all parts of the city. It was worth while making the journey if only to see the remarkable audience packed into the vast theatre, where the performance went on for four or five hours without a break. The prices of admission were extremely low, for the poorer people could have a seat in the gallery for threepence and a place in one of the stage boxes cost only two or three shillings.

How the theatre came into existence is quite a romantic story. A poor boy named Samuel Lane tramped all the way from his native Devon to London and found work in the theatre. He managed to save some money, and in 1856 he built the Britannia Theatre, which he managed so well and where he gave such good value for money that he became quite prosperous. When he died in 1871 he left the theatre to his wife, Sara Lane, and she controlled it until her death in 1899, when she left £160,000 – all made out of one theatre.

The Britannia pantomimes were wonderful entertainments and differed from the kind of thing to be seen elsewhere. For one thing they were never founded upon the usual subjects, but, like the old-fashioned pantomimes, they always had an original theme. In fact, the old type of entertainment was continued long after the other theatres had abandoned it. The Harlequinade, the transformation scene and much of the traditional fun were always to be seen. To the last the Harlequinade was regarded as a most important feature, and when it began to decline at other theatres and when any kind of Clown was considered suitable elsewhere only the best was considered good enough for the Britannia.

The pantomimes were never remarkable for pageantry and vast processions and splendid costumes. The strong points were plenty of boisterous fun, good scenery and elaborate effects and such features as appealed as much to the children as to the grown-ups.

What were known as "chase" scenes were frequently introduced. In these scenes the characters would join in an exciting pursuit entailing much use of trap-doors, through which the acrobatic artists would make their surprising entrances by springing up into the air. The many members of the famous Lupino family, to which I will refer later, always took a prominent part on this kind of thing.

The Britannia staged pantomimes for more than sixty years and then its fortunes failed and it became a cinema many years ago. The old theatre was badly damaged during the air raids of the last war and is now a melancholy ruin.

Charles Dickens visited it during its heyday and saw the pantomime *Needles and Pins* and this is what he wrote about it:

"We began at half-past six with a pantomime – with a pantomime so long that before it was over I felt as if I had been travelling for six weeks. The Spirit of Liberty, a principal personage in the introduction, and the Four Quarters of the World came out of the Globe and discoursed with the spirit who sang charmingly. We were delighted to understand there was no liberty anywhere but among ourselves and we highly applauded the agreeable fact.

"In an allegorical way, which did as well as any other way, we and the Spirit of Liberty got into the Kingdom of Needles and Pins and found them at war with a potentate who called in his and their old arch enemy Rust, who would have got the better of them if the Spirit of Liberty had not in the nick of time transformed the leaders into Clown, Pantaloon, Harlequin and Columbine and a whole family of sprites."

In order to give you an idea of the kind of pantomime that used to be seen at this famous theatre let me provide an outline of one or two of its stories. Here is what happened in *The Old Man and the Ass; or, Robin Redbreast's Eleven Hungry Brothers*.

Old King Cole in the depths of the coal mine tells his subjects that the Silver Gnome is penetrating to their domain for the purpose of destroying them. The moment that his forces succeed in capturing the gnome by means of a fairy talisman the scene changes to the Palace of Silver and reduces the coal demons to the necessity of working in their place. In a later scene, the exterior of Daddy Redbreast's cottage, Robin announces that he has had a dream to the effect that if he can blow from a silver whistle he could have all he wishes in the world. On awakening, to his surprise he finds the whistle by his side. He puts it to the test and the friendly Silver Gnome transforms him into a dashing gallant. Daddy Redbreast, unaware of his son's progress, is obliged to take a pet donkey to the market for sale. Robin there rescues it from being sold and is carried off in triumph by the villagers and wins the hand of Jenny Wrenne, daughter of Sir Roger de Wrenne. After a fight with the evil influence he is betrothed and is clapped into prison, but a blast from the magic whistle turns the tables on the gnomes and ensures the triumph of virtue.

Then again there was *The Spider and the Fly; or, King Jokose of Go for 'em Castle.* In this complicated story Tarantula, the Demon Spider, after much intrigue, succeeds in carrying off Princess Bluebelle, which, of course, creates great consternation in Jokose's court and not less in the heart of her suitor Fidelio. There is a similar case for when Damaris, Fidelio's sister, meets Prince Dandytoff they, too, love at first sight. Fidelio undertakes to lead a rescue party to run the Spider to earth and release Bluebelle, but this is a task of no small difficulty, for Tarantula, it seems, has the power of magic spell and causes much confusion by disguising himself as a parrot and changing many of his opponents into other characters.

An expedition gets lost in the dismal swamp when Scorpion, jealous of his master Tarantula, comes to their aid and leads them to the haunt of Demon Spider, where Bluebelle has been changed into a fly. Here the Spider is chased, and some remarkable mechanical effects are introduced. Finally the Demon is defeated, and Fidelio and Dandytoff obtain possession of their brides.

That was typical of the kind of story to be seen at the Britannia Theatre. There was always plenty of fun and excitement and always a sound moral with a proper victory in the end for all the virtuous characters.

Right to the last Mrs. Sara Lane always insisted on performing some part in the pantomimes. Writing about her performance in *Rominagrobis; or the Tale (Tail) of a Cat* one newspaper said:

"To see her as Alane successfully defying baronial villainies with the aid of a magic umbrella and literally singing and dancing her way through the most critical situations was to be impressed with the notion that she must have swallowed the elixir of youth that plays so comical a part in the plot of the pantomime."

Rominagrobis, was the story of an enchanter transformed by the good fairy Joyeuse into a cat minus its tail.

"The tail," records one who saw the performance, "has a separate history and an independent existence and the possessor of it has magic power. To recover possession of his tail is the object of Rominagrobis, and to retain it the object of Fanfarinette, who has obtained it to work harm to those he hates and to further his ends with those he is supposed to love. The loss, pursuit and recovery of the tail constitute the *motif* of the pantomime, but at the Britannia it would have been impossible to work it out in less than twelve scenes occupying three-and-a-half hours."

The titles of other Britannia pantomimes included *The Black Statue*, *Queen Dodo*, *The Magic Dragon* and *King Klondyke*, and all of them gave full scope for the kind of fun in which the theatre specialised.

I have just mentioned the Lupino family, members of which so often took part in the Britannia pantomimes, and as some of the family were related to Mrs. Lane, this should be the appropriate place to tell something about them.

Like the Grimaldis and the Bolognas, the family originated in Italy, and for over three hundred years it has been continuously associated with the business of entertainment. There have been Lupino puppet-makers, tight-rope performers, acrobats, dancers, singers, comedians, costume designers, musicians, managers, wig-makers and what-not, but above all they have shone in pantomime generally and in the Harlequinade in particular.

The first time that the name "Luppino", as it was originally spelt, appeared in connection with an English entertainment is on a handbill of St. Bartholomew's Fair in September 1642. It announced that Signor Luppino would present "Bel and Dragon, newly arrived, besides several Jiggs, Sarabands and country dances". The various living members of the family – they include Barry, Wallace and Lupino Lane, all of them notable figures in pantomime – are descendants of this puppet-master.

There was a Georgius Charles Luppino born in 1683, who married a Charlotte Mary Estcourt. Their son Georgius Richard (1710), when quite young, was apprenticed to Rich the Harlequin and made his first stage appearance as a small Harlequin in *The Two Harlequins* at Lincoln's Inn Fields Theatre in 1718.

Throughout the eighteenth century one comes across Lupino after Lupino on the playbills, now as a dancing master, now as a scene-painter, now as a sprite, as, for instance Thomas William Lupino (1791–1859), who made his pantomime appearance at Covent Garden in that character in *Harlequin Tom; or, the Dominion of Fancy*.

George Hook Lupino (1816–76) was apprenticed to Tom Matthews the Clown and began his stage career as a "blue monkey" at Sadler's Wells Theatre in the Easter pantomime of *Harlequin and the Fair One with the Golden Locks; or, the Giant's Isle*.

From the earliest days of its existence the Lupinos were continuously connected with the Britannia Theatre. Five generations of the family appeared there. A Harlequinade cast in 1880 consisted of Arthur Lupino as Pantaloon, George Lupino as Harlequin, Harry Lupino as Ally Sloper* and George, jun., as Clown.

By the early seventies the Lupinos had become one of the most famous pantomime troupes in England, each member excelling in some particular character. George Lupino was exceptionally skilled as a dancer and "star" trap performer. In the Drury Lane pantomime of 1889 he turned a triple pirouette out of a "star" trap, winning a wager of £50. This trap work subsequently became one of the great assets of the family. A frequent visitor to Drury Lane when George Lupino was appearing there was King Edward, who was particularly interested in the working of the "star" trap. It is said that he used to stand underneath the stage and watch Lupino as he disappeared down one trap and was shot up ten feet in the air from another.

George Lupino, who died in 1932, was indeed a grand old man of pantomime, and he was England's oldest Clown when, not long before his death, he arranged and took part in his last Harlequinade at the Theatre Royal, Birmingham, the very theatre in which he had been born. His eldest son Barry was the Harlequin on that occasion.

He came on in his old Clown's dress and carried on with surprising vigour until he came to the old familiar business of the red-hot poker. Then he handed the poker to the policeman, saying: "Take it; I've finished."

When he addressed the audience many of them, as at the retirement of Grimaldi, were in tears.

"I was more nimble when I first wore these," he said pointing to the wig and his shoes. "I was born somewhere near this spot, and now I'm here with my son standing by me and my grandson in front. I hope the great Producer of all will shower His best blessings upon you." Then he left the stage for the last time.

There have been many other families who have provided several generations of pantomime performers, but in these

* A popular character in a once very popular comic weekly.—AUTHOR

days there is not so much encouragement to continue in the line, and so many members of these families have taken up some other part of theatrical business.

Another theatre where pantomime of a type somewhat similar to those of the Britannia were staged was the Grecian Theatre in City Road. It was one of the most famous homes of pantomime in London, but it was demolished many years ago.

It was opened by George Conquest (whose real name was Benjamin Oliver) in 1851, and he was the founder of another remarkable pantomime family, most of the members of which specialised in acrobatic animal impersonation.

George Conquest himself was a supreme master of pantomime. He wrote them and he appeared in them himself and they always provided opportunities for the kind of nimble acrobatics in which he excelled. He was particularly agile as a sprite, and it is said he could jump higher than any artist has ever been able to accomplish. He would sing, dance, vanish through trap-doors, leap through a window and reappear in the twinkling of an eye. I have been told by an old playgoer that pantomime was never so exciting as at the Grecian.

Conquest was a wonderful impersonator not only of birds and animals, but of such inanimate things as turnips and of every other kind of queer character that used to figure in the fantastic pantomimes for which his theatre became so notable.

"A Grecian pantomime must necessarily allow the Conquests to be all over the stage at once, to disappear and reappear at the most unexpected times and in the most unlooked for places, to take desperate headers everywhere, to leap overhead like flying squirrels, and generally set in defiance the laws of physics as applied to the human form divine," said the *Daily Telegraph* of *Harlequin Roly-Poly* in 1877.

The story of this pantomime turned upon the desire of various personages to gain possession of a magic umbrella lost by Queen Gloria, the finder of which would presumably gain also her coveted hand. The candidates for the prize included representatives of all the elements as well as human characters. The chief of them, and finally the lucky one, was Roly-Poly, a water-sprite who was liberated from the interior of a roly-poly pudding, where by magic power he had been confined.

This character, of course, was played by George Conquest, and it enabled him to show his special agility now in the air, now in the bowels of the earth, now in the depths of the sea. He assumed many disguises, including those of a parrot and a dwarf, and with his son went through one of those amazing fights which were a speciality at the Grecian Theatre.

Describing his impersonation of a parrot, one writer said: "As a bird he was fearfully and wonderfully made, and he should be seen by all curious in ornithological matters. It yawns like a sluggard, talks like an orator, winks, like (as an American would perhaps call) a knowing cuss, is no mean dancer, can roar as gently as any sucking dove, can hold his own as a vocalist in solo, duet or chorus. It is without doubt the most remarkable bird the world has yet seen."

George Conquest, jun., who was born in 1837, developed acrobatic talent even greater than that of his father. In *The Devil on Two Sticks* in 1861 he used twenty-nine traps for his dizzy feats. No wonder that during his career he broke nearly every bone in his body in performing his leaps and jumps.

The last pantomime seen at the Grecian Theatre was *Hokee Pokee, the Fiend of the Fungus Forest; or, the Six Links of the Devil's Chain,* and it appears to have lived up to its splendid title. In the character of Hokee Pokee, George Conquest, jun., assumed all sorts of wonderful shapes, appearing now as a demon with glittering fans springing from his limbs and opening and closing at will; now as a vampire bat with glaring eyes and monstrous wings very much like the real article, and now as a porcupine with a multitude of quills.

This porcupine, it is said, took three years to make and was composed of over 2,500 separate pieces, each piece having a separate movement.

When the Grecian Theatre had to close George Conquest, jun., went over the water to the Surrey Theatre, a large house with a fine and long history that stood until quite recent years at the end of Blackfriars Road. There he made its pantomimes even more notable than they had been in the past. The first pantomime there was *Harlequin and the Witch of Ludlow*, which was produced in 1809. The theatre was burnt down in 1865 and when it was rebuilt it was always a popular home of pantomime. It was there, as I have described, that Dan Leno scored his early successes before being engaged at Drury Lane.

At the Surrey Theatre George Conquest's all-round talent as actor, manager, dramatist and acrobat had plenty of scope. When he died in 1901 his son Fred ran the theatre, and he was succeeded by his brother George. Arthur, another brother, was in *Sinbad* at Drury Lane in 1906, and he appeared there in many later pantomimes. George Conquest, great-grandson of the original, played Goose at the Surrey in 1921 and, making a speciality of that notable bird, appeared in many pantomimes until quite recent years.

The Surrey Theatre, after many changes and vicissitudes, finally closed its doors in July 1925, and was demolished in 1935, when the site was acquired for extensions by the Royal Eye Hospital.

Another vanished theatre was the Pavilion, Mile End, which was often proudly described as "the Drury Lane of the East". That lingered for many years as an empty ruin until it was destroyed during the wartime air raids.

Yet another theatre destroyed during the war was the Standard, Shoreditch, which was long owned by the Douglass family. The pantomimes there, says Albert Douglass, the historian of the family, "were delightfully written, dramatically constructed and played with a sincerity that would probably astound many modern comedians who, forgetting they are paid to amuse the audience, are sometimes more concerned with amusing each other".

John Douglass, who died in 1874, was for twenty-five years in management at the Standard. His first part in pantomime was as an imp. After much hard work in many theatres, he became the owner of the Marylebone Theatre, and later on he built the Standard, which was opened in 1867.

Douglass knew everything about the production of pantomime, for he was his own author, designer, modeller and producer. Other members of his family painted the scenery. His pantomime books were not very notable, but on his vast stage he gave his public plenty of spectacle and fun. After the Douglass family the Standard passed into the hands of Andrew Melville, father of the Melville brothers, who later on owned the Lyceum Theatre.

Another theatre with a long and interesting history was Sadler's Wells, once the home of Joseph Grimaldi. Situated in a poor part of London, its productions were never very elaborate or expensive, but many of the foremost Clowns appeared there during the palmy days of the Harlequinade. It had many ups-and-downs of fortune until it became a music hall in 1891. Then it was closed, and for years was a derelict ruin, until it was demolished to make way for the present fine theatre, notable for its ballet and opera.

In its early days the Adelphi Theatre, in the Strand, was famed for its pantomimes. The custom waned, and it was not until 1908 that the ancient glory was revived with *Cinderella*, which Robert Courtneidge, a manager from Manchester, staged with great taste and splendour. In fairylike charm it has perhaps rarely been surpassed. According to all accounts few things more beautiful in pantomime were ever seen than the transformation of Cinderella's kitchen into a wonderful palace of shimmering whites, greys and mauves.

The Princess's Theatre in Oxford Street was at one time famous for its pantomimes. This historic house, which was situated near the premises of Messrs. Waring & Gillow, remained empty for many years, until it was enclosed by other buildings and finally demolished.

Other famous pantomime houses of the past include the Royal Victoria (now the Old Vic, which at the time of writing is out of use as the result of war damage), the Elephant and Castle, which was demolished some years ago, the Royal West London in Chapel Street, Edgware Road, Astley's (later known as Sanger's) in Westminster Bridge Road, near St. Thomas's Hospital, which managed to combine pantomime with circus entertainment, and the Grand, Islington, which has been a cinema for many years.

Provincial theatregoers are very indignant if you suggest that all the best pantomime has been confined to London. They have good reason, for in the past the provincial theatres have been just as active in production, and with their own individuality and producers have often drawn admiring visitors from London.

A whole volume might be devoted to their records. Not only have Manchester, Liverpool, Birmingham, Leeds, Glasgow and Edinburgh had their admirable achievements, but such smaller towns as Brighton and Exeter would have to be taken into account if a full and complete history came to be written.

Such theatres as the Royal at Manchester (now a cinema), the Alexandra, Liverpool, the old Theatre Royal and the later Princes at Bristol (destroyed by bombs during the raids of 1940), the Royal at Birmingham, and the Alexandra in the same city (which invariably has the longest run in England), and the Grand Theatre, Leeds, all have interesting histories, about which volumes might be written.

16

Fun at the Lyceum Theatre

WHEN Drury Lane gave up the long-honoured custom of an annual pantomime the Lyceum Theatre became the acknowledged centre of the Christmas entertainment in London, and it worthily maintained the tradition for many years. In fact, as far as pleasing the younger theatregoers was concerned I don't think there has ever been anything better than the good, rousing, bustling, jolly kind of entertainment that this fine old theatre provided.

From its early days the Lyceum (which is best noted for the fact that it was the home for many years of Sir Henry Irving) was associated on and off with the production of pantomime. At one time the pantomimes there were under the direction of Oscar Barrett, who, in 1893, even outrivalled Drury Lane with his production of *Cinderella*, in which that lovely actress Ellaline Terriss (Lady Hicks) became the talk of London, because she made the sweetest of heroines.

Mr. Barrett's pantomimes were notable for their charming music, for the avoidance of what many parents deemed to be the vulgarity of music-hall humour and for prettiness and charm instead of extravagance and unnecessary display.

But it was when the brothers Melville took over the theatre that the real era of Lyceum pantomime began. They were men of great experience in the theatre and in all their long control they never had a failure. They knew exactly what their public liked and they never failed to provide it in full and generous measure. Grown-up playgoers sometimes complained of the lack of artistic taste displayed in the scenery and costumes, but that sort of thing passed unnoticed by the children, who always revelled in the rollicking fun and the slapstick nonsense which was never missing.

I have seen hundreds of pantomimes and in many different

theatres, but to my mind there never was anything quite like the opening night at the Lyceum. It was a theatre which looked exactly as a theatre should look – a vast house of gold and red plush and velvet, blazing with light from every tier. It was a perfect setting for pantomime. It was a rare sight to see that huge theatre with its large pit and its immense gallery filled with happy, eager and excited play-goers, among whom there were always hundreds of children, all waiting impatiently for the curtain to rise.

And when at length it rose, and when the buzz of excitement came to a sudden hush, what wonders, what delight and what fun were disclosed!

Let me try to give you a general impression of a typical performance of – it may be *Dick Whittington*, *Beauty and the Beast* or *Puss in Boots* – but the subject hardly matters.

First, on a mysteriously darkened stage with pale green spotlight to pick out the evil character, the Witch or Demon King, proclaiming his or her wicked designs against the Principal Boy or Principal Girl, and the timely entry of the Fairy Queen, who, to our delight, proposes to defend the hero and heroine against all such evil plans. The Demon King retires baffled, but vowing that he will not be deterred in doing his worst.

The scene changes to some brightly-lit, gaily-coloured, bustling market-place, filled with joyously singing inhabitants who have apparently nothing else to do but to gather round and raise their voices in song, to cheer the hero and to retire discreetly when the Principal Boy and Principal Girl obviously desire to be alone. Should the hero or heroine be disposed to sing, as is quite probable, the merry inhabitants are soon back in their places, ready to join in the chorus.

Of course, we all admire the handsome, dashing Principal Boy and fall in love with the Principal Girl, for that is a time-honoured habit of all true pantomime-lovers. This, of course, is all very well, and we dutifully enjoy it, but what we are really waiting for is the entry of the comedians, and here they come, sometimes with the aid of a curious-looking horse who, with its legs and disposition to dance, seems quite human. They are ridiculously arrayed and full of absurd antics from the moment of their entry. They are probably that superb couple Naughton and Gold, and a funnier pair you could hardly wish for, except perhaps Nervo and Knox. With good luck it might even be all four of them.

Another fun merchant enters, the Dame or Queen, probably represented by Clarkson Rose, a tall, gaunt and grotesque creature, wearing either gorgeous medieval-looking finery or shabby present-day dress. She is not without a certain dignity, but if a Queen, quite democratic in her manners and cheerfully ready to make the best of circumstances, even when, by one of those odd freaks of fortune which beset the monarchy in a pantomime, she is expected to take up residence in a council house.

And then, oh joy! a tall, ungainly fellow wearing tights striped in black and yellow like the colouring of a wasp, enters, gazing round with a look of wild surmise and a friendly word of greeting to the children. It is that superb, droll fellow, George Jackley, the man with thunder in his voice, elastic in his limbs and india rubber in his features.

Then you may be sure mischief and mirth will soon be redoubled. Soon they will be papering a room, or making a pudding in the royal kitchen, or performing other antics in which it is certain buckets of water are spilt all over the place, eggs are smashed regardless of cost, crockery is broken and everyone is smothered in flour or paste.

All this is splendid, and very splendid, too, the scene in which Clarkson Rose or George Jackley, with his hoarse, stentorious voice, persuades us to join in the chorus of some absurd, delightful song, the words of which, for our benefit, are displayed in large letters upon a sheet lowered from the flies.

Splendid also, if a little too long drawn-out, the ballets and the scenes in which lithe and amiable young ladies tie themselves into graceful knots for our delight, and more splendid yet – though perhaps regrettable, because it signifies that at last the pantomime is coming to an end – the Palace *finale*, when all the young ladies of the chorus group themselves at the bottom of the staircase in readiness to cheer the principals as they descend, all in their best clothes, and advance towards the footlights to receive our delighted applause.

Well, that is something like the sort of thing we used to see in the good old days at the Lyceum, and now alas! such jollity is only a memory.

The Melvilles constructed their pantomimes on rather novel lines. Long before the end of one pantomime they were busy on preparations for the following Christmas. They would first decide what the ballet scenes should be and then they prepared the designs for the Palace set. Not until these important matters were arranged did they decide upon the subject of the pantomime.

They used to write their "books" themselves, and they had a quality peculiarly their own. I have collected some delightful couplets from their joyous shows. I suppose you would call them verse or rhyme, but whatever they were they always expressed the cheerful inconsequence of pantomime. Niceties of metre or of rhyme never seemed to trouble them. If they couldn't think of the right word they invented one. For example, in *Beauty and the Beast* in 1937 there occurred this gem:

> Just swallow a dose of this potent philtre
> And your lover will never turn a jilter.

And again, when asked by the Fairy Queen against whom she directed her spite, the Witch replied:

> Who but the King who banished me that night
> Because my philtre and my necromancy
> Made no appeal to his anaemic fancy.

In *Puss in Boots* (1936) occurred this reproach:

> You foolish people – your tittle-tattle
> Is like the lowing of herds of cattle.

In the same pantomime the King gave this order to his cook:

> Cook, dissemble, take to the kitchen
> These animals, and woe betide the hag who
> Doesn't turn out a splendid stew or ragout.

In *Cinderella* (1931) there was Buttons' really heroic couplet:

> For you and Miss Cinders, here I'm content to have no wages
> But for your other daughters they fairly me enrages.

But the best of all couplets that I can recall occurred in *Dick Whittington:*

> As for you, you idle apprentice
> You really make me feel *non compos mentis!*

The Melvilles, I am glad to recall were strongly in favour of the retention of the good old-fashioned Harlequinade, and they always tried to give at least ten minutes of it, though they rarely succeeded in squeezing it into the first performance. Sometimes it did not appear until after the first week of the run.

"If we rang down the curtain without giving the kiddies their ten minutes of the red-hot poker stuff there would be a riot," Frederick Melville once declared.

One of the last productions at the Lyceum was seen by 300,000 people and it took £30,000 for its fortunate owners.

The last pantomime there was *Queen of Hearts* in 1939. After that the fine old theatre remained closed for several years, and when it reopened it was as a dance hall.

17

The Making of Pantomime

I HAVE now taken you through the whole history of pantomime since it became established in England, and I have shown how it has developed and have described the many changes it has undergone since it became the recognised form of entertainment for children at Christmas-time.

You will have seen how first nimble and sparkling Harlequin was the hero of the story; how he gave way to the jolly, mischievous Clown; how he, too – the idolised, fun-making favourite who was always the star and the most popular artist on the programme – had the fun taken from him and at length faded out of the picture to make way for the comedians. You have seen how many other things have disappeared – the "made-up" stories, the trap-door appearances and disappearances, the helter-skelter chases and the acrobatic displays of sprites and demon kings and, above all, the glorious, glittering transformation scenes which gave the scene-painters their finest opportunity of dazzling the eye with their glimpses of a Fairyland of tinselled delight.

These things are lost, and no doubt the disappearance of such features is to be regretted, particularly by old playgoers who will tell you that pantomime is not what it was in their childhood days. Only recently an old friend, whose memory of the theatre goes back much further than mine, wrote to me lamenting that the children of today will never know how glorious and how extravagant in spectacle and wonder were those pantomimes of Sir Augustus Harris and Arthur Collins. "I have seen hundreds of pantomimes during the last thirty to forty years," he says, "but I can assure you that not one of them comes within miles of any show that Drury Lane used to stage."

Well, you will find the same complaint echoed in every generation. Fifty years ago playgoers declared that there was nothing like the pantomimes of their boyhood to be seen and on every such occasion there have been many who have not hesitated to say: "Pantomime is dying." I have read such a statement in the newspapers of a hundred years or more ago.

Pantomime dying? Don't you be misled by what a few pessimists may say. As long as there are good children and kindly parents it will last as long as the Christmas pudding and the Christmas stocking. One might just as well talk of the death of Santa Claus.

True, pantomime has changed, and will, no doubt, continue to change as succeeding years introduce new ideas, but whatever the future may hold you may be sure that something which will be labelled Christmas pantomime and intended to divert young people will persist.

Even in the midst of wartime difficulties it flourished. We should be glad that the custom is indestructible, for in its topsy-turvy fun and its delightful absurdities it enshrines so much that is traditional. It is something utterly and completely British. Though, alas! the Harlequinade has vanished, much of its nonsense is still preserved in other ways. Let us hope that pantomime-writers will continue to honour the traditions that still linger. Let us hope that they will not forget to give us those lovely rhymed couplets of which the dialogue of pantomime was at one time wholly composed. They will surely never forget to give us plenty of spectacle and pageantry, heaps of comical animals, the riotous absurdities of comedians papering a kitchen and scattering the whitewash, of dames who do not spare the flour and the dough when they make puddings in their crazy kitchens.

And let them not forget to continue that time-honoured custom by which the Fairy Queen enters always from the right side of the stage and the Demon King from the left. To neglect this would be as wrong as it would be for the

Fairy Queen to forget to transfer her wand from the right hand to the left when her enemy enters. She does this, it has been said, "to protect her heart". But then, of course, every right-minded, well brought-up Fairy Queen should be aware of that.

Years ago a writer laid down the rules that should be observed in constructing an ideal pantomime. He said: "There must be songs, there must be a ballet; there should be some sufficient reproduction of a fairy-tale to be recognisable by the children; there should be scope for the impossible, the absurd and the grotesque and there should be a full stage and plenty of spectacle. The songs should be tuneful, the dances should be exhibitions of grace and skill, the ballet should be a harmony of movement. The transformation scene should be as beautiful as it can be made. Above all, the drollery should be droll and the fun should be funny."

Well, apart from the regrettable disappearance of the transformation scene, most present-day pantomimes manage to observe these excellent rules. They compose an admirable prescription, and I am sure that our leading producers do their best to observe them.

Pantomime producers, you should know, are generally styled "pantomime kings", and happily there are several of them in the field, chief among them being Mr. Tom Arnold, Mr. Prince Littler, Mr. Francis Laidler and Mr. Bertram Montague. Most of them each produces at least half a dozen pantomimes every Christmas; sometimes it is as many as ten. The preparation of pantomime, in fact, is quite an industry, and the work goes on throughout the year. For as fast as a pantomime "king" has presented his batch of shows in different towns and cities one Christmastide he is ready to begin his preparations for the next.

A pantomime "king" once told me: "As soon as Christmas is over I start touring the country and seeing other people's shows for likely artists. During the summer I visit the seaside, listening to the concert parties and hearing what tunes are applauded the most. For the song makes the pantomime. One of the first things I do is to make a note of the tunes I hear the boys whistling in the street. I take particular stock of the tunes that are popular in Blackpool and Douglas, for those that are popular there today are the rage in London tomorrow. In spite of the popularity of pantomime among adults I consider them last when putting on my shows. I allow myself to be governed almost entirely by children. Experience has taught me that if I can please them the success of the pantomime is assured.

"Children are not only discerning critics, but are jealous guardians of the highest tradition. If I tamper with a story, interpose a new scene or introduce some novelty I am in danger of stirring up a hornet's nest of angry young critics. Once I took a liberty or two in presenting *Dick Whittington* at Manchester and I received letters of protest from many children."

All the pantomime producers keep large staffs engaged solely on making scenery and costumes for the Christmas shows. Mr. Prince Littler is very proud of Pantomime House, his headquarters in Birmingham. There you find workshops of every description, and one of the busiest is that controlled by Mrs. P. L. Wright, who has adopted the curious name of "Physhe", which you may have seen on your programme. For last year's productions she had 15,000 clothing coupons to dispose of in purchasing the necessary articles and materials. With them she had to provide 4,000 dresses – to say nothing of curtains, shoes and tights for six pantomimes. She employs fifty girls in making and repairing costumes, embroidering, making buttonholes and sewing on spangles. "Before the war," she said, "you could make a crinoline for £10. Now you are lucky if you can do it for £120. Satin once cost us four shillings a yard. Now – if you can get it – it costs anything from £4 to £5 a yard."

Mr. Bertram Montague has his pantomime factory in London, where twenty-four men and women are continuously employed. He will tell you that it once cost £35 to provide a principal boy with a wardrobe. Now the cost is more than £100.

One of the busiest of these pantomime workers is a clever man named Ernie Sly, who is responsible for all the woodwork required for Mr. Tom Arnold's pantomimes. Throughout the summer he and his men – as many as twenty at the peak – are busy with hammer, saw and plane on every bit of wood they can obtain at the Hove workshop. It has to supply pantomimes from Brighton in the south to Glasgow in the north.

Some of the workshops I have mentioned make their own "props" – that is to say the various odds and ends that are used in the pantomime. It may be anything from a red-hot poker, a giant frying-pan or a tempting looking (if over-sized) roast turkey or leg of mutton, to a giant's head, Cinderella's coach or a crazy-looking motor-car. Being magicians in a way, these skilful people are ready to produce anything of that kind required.

One of the most interesting branches of pantomime production is the workshop where animal and bird skins and masks are made. I once paid a visit in a dingy part of London to one of these establishments and I can tell you it was a weird sight.

Round the walls in tiers I saw an array of donkeys' heads, skulls, carnival masks, the fearsome heads of ogres and giants of every conceivable kind. The floor was littered with such awesome looking things as papier-mâché croco-diles, monster rats and mice, horses, cows and mules. As I picked my way among these grotesque creatures the chief magician told me that he was ready to make cows that cry with most realistic tears, horses that wink and yawn, dragons that belch fire and puff smoke through their nostrils and any other fearful or realistic kind of animal that you can think of.

He produces many cat skins for the impersonators who frolic in such a lifelike way in *Puss in Boots* or *Dick Whitting-ton*. The artificial fur is hand-woven on a century-old knitting loom. Each hair has to be separately adjusted and when the skin is finished it fits the wearer like a glove.

He is very clever in making the outer part of the goose that lays the golden eggs. I learned that the building-up of a goose is one of the most difficult of jobs, for every feather has to be stitched on separately, a job that occupies a man for three weeks. The feathers are obtained from the plumage of swans and turkeys and are each fixed with wire. The result is most lifelike. A goose's outfit costs about £40 to make, but that of a cat or monkey only about half as much. Most cat impersonators provide their own skins.

Mr. Mayers, the owner of this wonder workshop, told me many other interesting things. He told me that he obtained many of his ideas for pantomime animals and birds from the drawings in comic papers and I learnt from him that an animal is built up on a framework of wire or basket-work, covered with paper or leather, on which the skin, made of "animal baize" (a trade term for a woollen material), is sewn on.

"Fred Conquest," he said, "was the finest goose that ever trod the stage, and I suppose the best pantomime cat was Charles Lauri. He used to put on his cat's skin here and he would jump on to a shelf just like the real thing."

I can vouch for the real, pussy-like manners of Mr. Lauri myself, for I can remember as a child seeing him run all round the balcony of the theatre in a most feline way and to the intense delight of the children when he paused to let them stroke his sleek back.

By the way, I can tell you that Mr. Mayers followed his father in the business, which was started in 1821, and that provides us with one more example of the way in which pantomime tradition is carried on from one generation to another.

From all this you will probably get some idea of the amount of work entailed in providing you with your Christmas treat. When you come to think of it is really is remarkable how the work of so many different people is blended in the production of that delightful entertainment which you have so much enjoyed.

There are the writers of the pantomime or the people who revise an old "book" and bring it up to date with fresh jokes and new scenes; there are the composers of the songs, the conductors who arrange the different parts for the music and the musicians in the orchestra. There are the many artists engaged in the show, from the principal boy and girl, and the comedians to the innumerable people in the chorus and ballet. There are dances and ballets to arrange; there are what is known as "speciality turns" – acrobats, performing animals, jugglers and others who are introduced to give variety to the performance – there are the girls of the "flying ballet" who hover so gracefully over the stage and the watchful men behind the scenes who control the movements of the wires from which they are suspended. There are the dressmakers and costumiers who design and make the dresses; there are the people who make the "props". There are the scene-designers and the scene-painters and carpenters who carry out those designs. There are the stage-hands who work so swiftly and noiselessly in effecting the changes of scenery and the electricians who are responsible for arranging and controlling the lighting of the stage, which is always such an important matter in pantomime.

All these and many more are responsible for the attraction of the entertainment which, when you see it, flows so smoothly and without a hitch, each part of it moving with the accuracy of clockwork. Nothing more suggests the magic of pantomime than that an affair should run with such precision when the curtain rises on the first performance.

It seems more wonderful still when you realise how quickly the whole pantomime is arranged and put together by the producer. It is all done in a matter of four or five weeks. Of course, scene-painters and costume-workers have been hard at work for many months in preparing their part of the pantomime, but not until towards the end of

November do the artists engaged begin their preparations.

Come with me and let us have a glimpse of the sort of thing that goes on. Let us say it is a pantomime for the Coliseum. It all looks very quiet outside the theatre, but once inside you are in the midst of a bustle of activity. It is a vast theatre with many large rooms and in every one of them you will find something going on. In one room you will find twenty or thirty people lustily singing to the accompaniment of a piano. They are rehearsing their parts for the opening chorus which in a few weeks' time they will be singing as the curtain rises on the market-place of Some-where-or-other. They go over some of the bars of the song again and again. It is a task to test the patience.

In a smaller room nearby Prince Charming or Dick Whittington, or whatever hero that good-looking young lady in the mink coat will shortly swaggeringly represent on the stage, is running through her duet with another pretty girl who is going to be Cinderella or Alice Fitz-warren. From another part of the theatre comes a rhythmic tap-tap, the sound of dancing feet, for there the ballet is going through its steps.

Now come through the darkened theatre, where the vacant stall seats are shrouded in white dust-sheets, towards the stage, which looks strange and bare in the faint lighting. There are carpenters, stage-hands and electricians at work, but the noise they make and the constant shifting of pieces of scenery, the activities of the electricians manipulating entanglements of wiring, is no apparent hindrance to the rehearsal of other sections of the pantomime artists. Far down the stage in front of the footlights, seated round a table, are four men discussing some important matter. Now and again one of them will get up and go through some comical motions, at which his companions will laugh approvingly. They are the comedians, and much of the funny business at which you, too, will laugh when they assume their pantomime disguises, is left to them to invent.

At the sides of the stage the men who control the graceful

movements of the flying ballet are arranging the wires from which the fairies are suspended. It is a rather expert business and, as you may imagine, only lightweight girls are picked out to take part in the mid-air ballet. The wires are attached to hooks concealed beneath their fairy costumes and for each fairy there is a man to pull and release the wires as they flit to and fro.

But I have forgotten one most important section of the pantomime company. I mean the children who are always an important feature of the production. There may be a dozen or as many as twenty or thirty of them, and I don't suppose anybody in the show enjoys the work so much or puts so much spirit into the performance. With their bobbed hair – for that is generally insisted upon – they look like sisters of one huge family.

Many stars of pantomime have begun in this way. Most of them come from theatrical training schools, where they are taught dancing, and they all seem happy and eager in their work. The lot of these children has changed considerably since the early days of pantomime. Victorian writers used to draw pathetic pictures of what little waifs, shivering in their poor clothing, had to endure. Most of them in those far-off days were the children of ill-paid stage-hands, and they or their parents were glad to receive the shilling or so that was considered sufficient reward for a performance.

Nowadays children playing in the West End are paid about £5 a week during the run of the pantomime and they are well looked after. They are escorted to and from their homes and every care is taken to ensure that they get their proper meals and have sufficient rest between performances. When they are not on the stage they must remain in their dressing-rooms, for it would never do for them to roam about and get in the way of all the busy folk behind the scenes.

From all this you will understand that pantomime at the beginning is a rather scattered business and the ordinary onlooker who has witnessed such scenes as I have described is bewildered by what seems to him to be a gigantic muddle and confusion. But when each section has learnt the part which it is to play, the pantomime begins to assume a definite shape, and very soon it is necessary to assemble all the pieces of a complicated jig-saw puzzle. Then it is surprising how the whole thing fits together.

About a week before the first performance the company is rehearsing the complete pantomime. The rough edges are smoothed out, and finally, when the costumes, all bright and fresh-looking in their gay colours, are ready to be worn there is a dress rehearsal, to which it is often the custom of the kindly managements to invite hundreds of the poorer children whose parents cannot afford such a Christmas treat. It goes like clockwork, if not with that smoothness right from the opening scene to the final chorus which a good producer will secure for the first exciting public performance.

London has now no acknowledged centre for Christmas pantomime as in the old days, when Drury Lane set the standard of production and, in name at least, was probably familiar to every child. To be taken there and to see the wonderful entertainment that it provided was the ambition of every boy and girl who had any notion of what fun and delight pantomime could afford.

When that ancient custom was abandoned it became the turn of the Lyceum Theatre which, for many years, set out a splendid feast aimed mainly at giving delight to the young folk. When the doors of that historic theatre closed, however, there was no longer any fixed home for the seasonable entertainment. Pantomime was likely to bob up at any theatre in the West End. Every year it has found a home somewhere or other within the magic circle, whether at the Coliseum, the Casino, the Princes or the London Palladium, which staged its first pantomime – a sumptuous, glittering and highly successful presentation of *Cinderella* – at Christmas-time, 1948.

In fact, pantomime that year set up some new records. In

London and throughout the country there were nearly 200 productions. The most popular subject, as usual, was *Cinderella* of which there were thirty-seven representations, followed by *Dick Whittington* with twenty-one, *The Babes in the Wood* with nineteen, *Aladdin* with eighteen, *Mother Goose* with sixteen and the rest divided between the other favourite subjects.

Among the grown-ups fashions may change. Other forms of entertainment may come and go. But children of every generation remain loyal to the heroes and heroines of the fairy-tale, and nothing can give them more delight than to see their old favourites going through their familiar adventures amid the splendour and the frolic of Christmas pantomime.

THE END